Western

Culture

A Guide

for Asian Students

Also by Bill Sinunu

Evolving Globe Series:

Business —

Sales Evolution
HR Evolution
Student Evolution

Travel —

Living Without Borders

Details at BillSinunu.com.

About Bill Sinunu

BILL SINUNU, MA, a University of Chicago-trained Master Facilitator and author of two best-selling books, is a cross-cultural speaker, trainer and consultant. In the Evolving Globe Series, look for business books *Sales Evolution*, *HR Evolution* and *Student Evolution*.

Additionally, he is a Ted Talk presenter and board member at Purdue University's Center for International Business Education and Research. The former airline executive offers culturally insightful keynotes, training and coaching for his corporate and university clients.

Sinunu, who is tri-lingual, is a former interpreter for the US Department of Immigration/Customs and was appointed to a U.S. Department of Health and Human Services task force.

Praise for Bill Sinunu

"Bill invites you to participate in his worldly travels and consider the scope of a wildly diverse planet."

Greg Kinnear
Actor, Academy Award nominee and Sinunu fan

"Sinunu traverses cultures and individuals—and the outcome is a mosaic of thoughts and feelings that is at once both universal and personal. A rare feat."

Tal Ben-Shahar, PhD
Professor – Harvard University

Western Culture

A Guide for Asian Students

First Edition

By Bill Sinunu M.A.

William Sinunu, 2014, Publisher

Table of Contents

Introduction

My hope is that any Asian student, who desires an understanding of the adjustments required in order to succeed in a Western academic environment will benefit from *Western Culture*. *Western Culture* addresses cultural transitions as a foundation for not only a student's academic life, but prepares students professionally for a successful career in what has become a highly interactive global marketplace.

Although the material for this book is designed for all those who come from the Far East (China, Japan, Korea, Taiwan), the number of Asian students wishing to study in the West are mostly Chinese. In fact, nearly half of all international applications to US graduate schools are from Chinese students. Although the concepts of this book are applicable to a number of cultures (such as Taiwanese students wishing to study in Australia or Korean students planning to study in the United Kingdom), I have elected to minimize confusion and maximize understanding by limiting the book's examples to Chinese students seeking an American education.

As stated, the increase in Chinese pursuing higher education is more than just notable; the number of Chinese students wishing to study in the West has simply exploded. What do we make of this upswing? The ongoing surge in Chinese student enrollments can be attributed to several contributing factors that are covered below.

For one, barriers for Chinese students to travel and study abroad have been relaxed, so it is easier for Chinese students to obtain student visas and travel to and from China. As a result, large numbers of Chinese students have studied abroad over the last few years, and that trend is expected to continue.

Also contributing to the surge of Chinese enrollment is the fact that in China a Western college education is regarded as desirable. An education in the West is seen as opening career doors both in China and abroad.

Of all the reasons for the increase in Chinese enrollment, the next one resonates for those of us who are eager to facilitate understanding between cultures. Although the Chinese educational system, built upon heavy levels of testing and memorization, has many beneficial qualities, the American approach to learning, which emphasizes creativity, innovation, teamwork and problem solving is popular amongst global business leaders.

One of the main reasons an American education is so popular in China is because a Western academic experience is seen as an opportunity to explore and blossom. Students will be in an environment that fosters empathy, imagination and resilience. In general, an American education provides an opportunity for Chinese students to gain not only a quality academic skill set, but also a social competence required to thrive in the global marketplace.

So, when Chinese students come to a multicultural and interactive US campus, how does their cultural background affect their experience? For some it can be a difficult adjustment. Socially, it can be a lonely and challenging time. However, for others, it is a time of growth and exploration. This book opens doors for Chinese students by preparing newcomers for a more confident, informed and culturally astute experience abroad.

The first chapter establishes the framework for the book and describes common scenarios experienced by Chinese students, and outlines strategies on how to cope, adjust and thrive in a new cultural setting. There is also an exploration of whether or not an international education is the right course of action for students.

This book is the Asian student's guide to success. It provides the soft skills and interaction tools for an insightful and rewarding stay in the US. Readers will have a clear understanding of Western communication styles and become very familiar with obstacles typically encountered by Chinese students. More importantly, they will be well-acquainted with essential strategies in order to overcome hurdles and succeed in American classrooms and multinational boardrooms.

Chapter 1

A Challenge: Are you Jiang or Wei?

Jiang is a typical Chinese student who achieved a very high score on his SAT college entrance examination. As an incoming freshman, he sits quietly by himself either in the library cubicle or at the back of the class. He has only Chinese friends and thinks sports and parties and other such social events are beneath him. He becomes very depressed and longs for China. He is completely disconnected from Western culture and uninterested in America.

There are many Chinese students in the U.S. who are just like Jiang. Citing data compiled by the 2013 Overseas-Returned Graduate Recruitment Report and university statistics, the *South China Morning Post* of Hong Kong reports that one in four

Chinese students attending Ivy League universities in the U.S. end up dropping out. The study said that while students exhibited high academic achievement in their home country, many found it difficult to adjust and adapt to the new environment, citing problems like language barriers and differences in the education system.

Wei (or "Wendy"—the name she goes by in the US) has a different mindset from Jiang. She thinks the social skills she is learning by interacting with other non-Chinese students are just as important as her academic education. She values the process of learning others' ways of thinking, creativity, communication, the soft skills you can never learn from books but rather from immersion in the culture and day-to-day interactions. She attends social events on campus and along with Chinese friends, has a multicultural social network and an American roommate. Since coming to the US, Wei has developed much stronger communication skills and has become more independent and confident.

The questions introduced by these two different scenarios are important. Students need to ask:

1. What will be the best approach for me?

2. Knowing myself, am I more likely to be like Jiang or Wei?

The challenge for the Chinese student is one of accepting that there is a choice. The choice is based on:

a) what approach will best honor the student's goals and

b) which option is comfortable.

Only the student can decide what is the most comfortable or productive option. Before making any decisions, there is more information to consider, such as whether or not a Western education is a good investment for the future.

Return On Investment (ROI)

ROI or *return on investment* is a common term in American business. The term refers to a benchmark to test if an individual or company should invest the time, energy, money and other resources into a project. This approach can also be used when evaluating whether a Western education is a good investment for Chinese students.

A Western education is expensive. It will cost a great deal of money not only in tuition costs, but living and travel expenses. So, it makes sense to ask the question:

Is this a good investment of money, time and energy?

Let's look at the data. Many multinational corporations in China seem to prefer *hai gui* applicants. *Hai gui* literally translates to "sea turtles," but it is a Mandarin term for those returning to China after being abroad. In particular, *hai gui* is often used to describe those who have received a Western education and then returned to China for career purposes. *Hai gui* are often respected in China. For example, a partner and recruiter for L.E.K. in Shanghai claims *hai gui* employees tend to speak English fluently, are significantly mature and notably skilled to function and interact socially with all types of people.

However, a survey of Chinese employers found that 70% of Chinese employers say they will not give preferential treatment to *hai gui* candidates and 8% say they actually prefer not to hire *hai gui*. Many within this survey said they find *hai gui* salary expectations too high and since the *hai gui* have been abroad for several years, they do not have the personal connections (*guan xi*) their Chinese counterparts have made (see the networking chapter for tips on how to overcome this obstacle.). However, many international business analysts foresee a number of Chinese companies expanding internationally and acquiring American and other Western corporations—thus, creating a huge opportunity for *hai gui*.

Recommendation

If Chinese students immerse themselves in the Western culture and learn the soft skills of interacting in a global community with students from all around the world, the investment in a Western education is worth it. In other words, if students go to university in the US thinking more like Wei than Jiang, they will have a greater chance of success in or out of China.

Based on the success of others, if Chinese students graduate from the West with the following skill sets, they will be a highly desirable candidate in China and other parts of the world:

1. A communication skill set that allows students to function within international communities

2. A cross-cultural sensitivity and ability to comfortably interact in multicultural environments

3. A confidence, independence and vision to lead Chinese and multicultural teams

All of these traits are highly sought after by both Chinese and international companies. In reality, these multicultural social skills are as important as or even more important than the academic knowledge obtained. Many Chinese students have remained in China and have solid educations, but have not had the *hai gui* cultural experience or social exposure.

For example, many young, educated Chinese professionals have never lived away from their family's home. Although these individuals often benefit from strong family ties, they may be at a disadvantage in the global economy as a result of limited international social exposure or the confidence gained by living on their own. In addition, many have studied English for years and do well on English exams, but do not have the ability to comfortably carry on a conversation in English. Although many languages are spoken in the international business community, English is the primary language and competence in the language will help Chinese entrepreneurs not only thrive globally, but function in key emerging English-speaking Asian markets like the Philippines, Malaysia and Singapore.

In general, *hai gui* have a distinct advantage over those who are not educated abroad. *Hai gui* have the skill set to excel without constant supervision and can become competitive in the international labor market, thus commanding salaries on par with international experts in their field.

So, is a Western education worth the

investment? The data indicates that it is—especially if one looks ahead to an increasingly global Chinese economy.

However, a student's level of success will depend on their approach. If students cope with the challenge of living in another culture by isolating themselves like Jiang, they will be missing out on one of the most important parts of their education. However, if they go abroad and attend a Western school with a mindset like Wei's, they will establish a foundation for a successful career and do extremely well.

Besides asking "am I Jiang or Wei?", one of the keys to establishing a foundation for success in Western academic and work environments is found in learning more about Americans in general. For that reason, the following chapter clarifies some Western norms, values and interaction styles while also comparing Chinese and American cultural communication mindsets.

Chapter 2

Understanding Americans

An Introduction to Western Norms, Values and Interaction Styles

A business book in today's marketplace has to include a chapter that outlines contrasting East and West mindsets. Although there are a number of differences between Chinese and American cultural approaches, as outlined in the following pages, the chapters following this one will provide strategies to bridge the gaps and build harmonious intercultural relationships.

Comparison of Chinese/American Cultural Communication Mindsets:

Keep in mind as you read the following comparisons that these scenarios will help you understand how to relate with Americans.

Chinese Collectivism *as compared to* American Individualism

Americans focus more on individual accomplishments and goals versus the Chinese priority of focusing on the group and what is best for all. In fact, a popular American adage that illustrates the American approach to life is "Every man for himself." Based on this adage, it would be easy to assume Americans are completely self-serving. It isn't necessarily that Americans don't care about others. Many do; however, the cultural mindset is that one takes care of their own individual needs first before considering the needs of others.

That sense of being an individual is evident in many parts of American life, including education. Students in a US university are expected to be independent and responsible. While there are some exceptions, in the US, American professors will not guide students individually through their studies. This is especially true when compared to the levels of help and support available in the Chinese educational environment. Many Chinese professors spend a considerable amount of individual time with students and work with them, much like a tutor. In the US, this does not happen. Tutors are available at an additional financial cost but professors do not provide that level of added help. Professors expect students to work individually and as a team member within their groups. Although professors provide office hours (typically a couple of hours a week) to meet with students, students are expected to ask only one or two questions and meet with the professor for a short time. In addition, on the graduate level, students can expect classes to move quickly, covering several chapters per week. It is not unusual for unannounced quizzes and tests to be given in order to insure students are keeping up with the material.

Chinese Hierarchy *as compared to* American Equality

The statement, "All men are created equal." is a strong part of the American history and is traced back to the Declaration of Independence. Yet, many observers of America and its society refute this statement. The reason for this can be found when looking at American society more closely: Many people have accurately identified disparities based on race, gender and social standing. But that reality does not consciously apply to the way most Americans approach business or academic interactions. In spite of disparities, it is still true that the statement, "All men are created equal." has a powerful impact on American thinking and applies to all parts of American life. As an example, when working in a group, Americans generally believe all members of a team are equal while the Chinese team members' culture is more conscious of and heavily influenced by factors like age, gender, social status and experience.

Since many academic projects are within a team or group setting, this cultural difference is important for Chinese students, attending college in the US, to know.

In an American classroom, everybody in a group is expected to participate. In many classes, part of a student's grade is based on their level of participation. With the American approach, all points of view are considered and respected regardless of age, gender or social status. This can be quite intimidating for Chinese students. Chinese students, who are often young and inexperienced, feel uncomfortable speaking out and voicing their opinion in the classroom. In addition, American students often appear aggressive because of their tendency to take charge and organize the group. However, once Chinese students get used to the new, fast-paced environment, most students adapt and thrive.

It's the same dynamic in the US business world. New as well as experienced employees are expected to voice their opinions. Participation is considered an opportunity to make a good impression and positions employees for promotion and leadership roles. As an example, in the US, there is a widely used saying—"You don't get a second chance to make a first impression." Participation creates opportunities to be noticed. By contrast, in China, young executives look to older, experienced male executives to decide if a working relationship will be established. In rare cases, those older executives are women, although the role of women in business is evolving and women are becoming more prominent in Chinese business. In the US, a leader of a team may be a) much younger, b) less experienced, or c) a female (or all the above). Factors such as age, experience and gender are considered less important in the US than China. Team leaders in American organizations are typically selected based upon their ability to lead, motivate, organize and manage people.

Within the American academic and business world, group leaders are often expected to speak in front of groups. This is very intimidating for most people, regardless of cultural background. But speaking in front of a large group can be particularly difficult for Asian students who have little public speaking experience and tend to be circular in thought process (discussed in detail shortly). We will talk more about public speaking in the upcoming chapters, but here is the first tip: Before speaking to a classroom or corporate group, map out what you are going to say and make your statement informative, relevant, clear and concise.

Chinese Relationship Priority *as compared to* American Information Priority

The Chinese business culture is focused initially on the relationship. Before embarking on the road to business, Chinese leaders want to get a strong sense of their new business partners. Americans immediately focus on the deal and information, i.e. questioning whether data supports a strategic initiative. The Chinese approach does not put as much emphasis on the actual deal or profitability potential (at the beginning of the relationship) but focuses more on individuals and their related personality traits. Even if Americans know little about their business partners, Americans will do business if the deal is seen as a profitable business decision. Chinese want to know if the people they are doing business with are reputable and to be trusted before thinking about money. Americans make business decisions solely on facts and rely heavily on ROI—return on investment. Although the Chinese consider business dealings based on fact, the culture also relies heavily on intuition and finding the right business partner.

Chinese Circular Thinking *as compared to* American Linear Thinking

Chinese are more circular and theoretical in their thought processes. Americans are very direct. As a result, there are often misunderstandings during interactions (such as public speaking and/or negotiations). Americans expect presentations to be short, direct and logical. The Chinese culture finds much learning and understanding comes from life experiences and letting a process slowly unfold. As a result, Chinese often find American presentations to be too simplistic and incomplete (not considering all the factors). Americans typically find Chinese presentations unclear and too detailed.

During the negotiation process, the following dynamic often arises. Fast moving and "linear thinking" Americans assume a speaking point has been agreed upon once it has been discussed and that part of the negotiation is settled and finished. But "circular thinking" Chinese often revisit negotiated points for further discussion. This is the point where negotiations often break down. American sales teams become confused and angry when the Chinese team wants to discuss an earlier point. Chinese negotiators become offended by the American team's anger and reluctance to further discuss earlier points within the agreement.

It's an example of cultural misinterpretation. During negotiations, a leader of the Chinese team may nod their approval or say "yes, I see" after an American has made their pitch. Americans may inaccurately interpret this act as agreeing to the terms the American is proposing. But, in reality, the Chinese leader is saying, "I understand what you are saying. It will be considered and we will talk about this again in the future."

To make the communication gap even more intense, American timing during negotiations is often out of step. Americans often make their pitch too quickly and early for the Chinese team. Even though the Chinese team hasn't decided if the US team is a suitable business partner, Chinese negotiators will respond with "yes, I see" to an American pitch because to respond any other way would feel rude. As a result, Americans feel negotiations are progressing quickly while the Chinese team hasn't even decided if they will enter negotiations.

As you can see, the negotiation process between the Chinese and American teams can be very confusing for both cultures. Once both teams are in negotiations, American sales teams are frustrated since the Chinese team often comes back to renegotiate points Americans believe have already been discussed, settled and agreed upon. At the same time, Chinese see American negotiators as rushing towards a deal, unwilling to discuss the proposed project in depth and hesitant to revisit topics previously discussed.

Chinese value "Seeking the Way" *as compared to* the American value of "Seeking the Truth"

Americans look for the "right" answer or decision and how to move the business deal along. The Chinese believe there is value in evaluating and learning from the journey. Chinese prefer to proceed slowly and pay keen attention to body language, unspoken communication and what "unfolds" along the way. Americans are focused primarily on the result and the quickest way to get there.

The fast-moving, quick-decision American approach is another adjustment for Chinese students. In group projects, there is often little time for extensive discussion or getting to know the interaction style of other team members. Western team members often appear bossy or overly aggressive. The natural non-confrontational cultural reaction for Chinese students is to become silent and withdrawn during overwhelming team conversations. This is another key element of cultural misunderstanding. Chinese consider American high participation levels overly aggressive and disrespectful. Americans consider Chinese lack of participation or silence to be a sign of disinterest or no opinion.

Chinese Bargaining *as compared to* American Fact and Logic

Although the negotiation process is not a cultural issue in the academic setting, it is very apparent in the business world. Americans believe in presenting their arguments logically and based on facts (cost, profit margins, etc.). While the Chinese do not abandon logic or devalue facts, the culture also believes in negotiation. Therefore, interactions between the cultures are often filled with long periods of silence (which typically make Americans very uncomfortable) and a lengthy negotiation process. The Chinese are comfortable with a long negotiation process. Americans are not.

Chinese leaders tend to prolong interactions and negotiations because the approach often results in the best deal. This strategy often works with impatient Americans who become quickly frustrated and present a more favorable package to Chinese negotiators in order to finalize a deal.

The American tactic often backfires since the Chinese team then has more favorable terms as a new benchmark to once again begin haggling. This approach can sever the relationship when frustrated American negotiators abandon the relationship and seek a new Chinese business partner.

This scenario can then take on an additional layer of frustration when Americans, refusing to acknowledge a culturally different negotiation style, find themselves in the same long, slow process they faced before—just with a different Chinese negotiating team.

Long Chinese Relationship Building Process *as compared to* Quick American Dealings

The Chinese business protocol is clear and proceeds with caution. Before establishing a business relationship, the general approach is one of making sure the potential business partners are trustworthy. A great deal of time is spent interacting with others to understand a sense of their background and motivation. There is no time limit or any sense of urgency to establish the relationship. Americans approach business in a much different way.

Americans value productivity and are accustomed to quick, decisive meetings. The individual personalities of the players are not typically important to Americans. As long as a deal can be struck and a contract signed, most Americans are not concerned with the other side's personality traits or values.

Not only are the priorities of each culture different, but also how each culture approaches the process is different. With little pressure and an unlimited timeframe, the Chinese team is constantly assessing those across the table. Typically, after each cross-cultural encounter, the Chinese delegation assembles and discusses observations of the individuals or team.

When Americans debrief, they usually discuss the terms of the deal, not individuals on the other team. This is particularly true for debriefing Americans after negotiations with an Asian team. Debriefs are almost completely about the deal since the Chinese team typically speaks little and Americans, in general, are not aware or conscious of non-verbal communication styles.

As one can imagine, this is yet another challenge for Chinese students attending a US university. Team projects are designed to be very short and it is common to work on one short project with a group of members and then work with a completely different team on the next short project. There is often little time to get to know individual personalities or working styles. It is a constant adjustment and Chinese students are pushed out of their comfort zones.

Chinese Formality *as compared to* American Informality

Although formality and protocol are signs of respect and proper etiquette in China, Chinese students will discover an informal academic and professional atmosphere in the US. Americans are known for being informal in their approach with each other and immediately sense they have built an "addressing each other by first names" friendly relationship—often from the first interaction. Believing this to be the best approach to make people comfortable, Americans feel it is appropriate to be informal. The informal approach is not a major issue in the academic world since students are comfortable calling each other by their first name. However, this can be an adjustment for students when addressing informal professors or administrators. While it's not necessarily the norm, students should not be surprised to meet a professor or college administrator who prefers to be called by his or her first name.

The lack of formality may feel out of place to Chinese students in both the American academic and professional world. For example, as fellow students joke and casually chat with the department head, Chinese students may feel that kind of behavior is disrespectful and inappropriate. Additionally, in the corporate world, many young Chinese may feel more comfortable addressing the boss formally (Mr. or Mrs.), limiting their conversations to work-related material and only speaking to the boss if the boss speaks to them first.

Chinese Draw On Intermediaries *as compared to* Americans Who Make Cold Calls

In America, "cold calls" are the norm. The term "cold call" is a term used to describe phone calls made in hopes of finding business. If a sales person can anonymously find an individual or company that needs the product or service and a deal can be struck, all is well even if the sales person doesn't know the customer. Many business deals in the US are between individuals who have spoken on the phone or corresponded via the Internet, but never personally met. As a result of the Chinese cultural norm of placing great value on the business relationship, most Chinese will only conduct business with others who a) they know or b) somebody, who they trust, knows.

This approach is not an issue for Chinese students in the university setting, but it may be an issue during internships. Based on the Chinese cultural norm, it may be uncomfortable to initiate a cold call and make a sales pitch to someone you have not met and have little knowledge of.

Full Authority *as compared* to Limited Authority

American sales representatives often have permission to individually strike a deal. American training programs focus on the product or service along with cost and profit margins. Although the

Chinese individual (or more often, individuals) who meet(s) with the American executive may have the same product knowledge, the Chinese executive(s) will rarely agree to a deal without consulting others on the team. Rather, in true collective form, the Chinese sales representative will report back with all the information and the group will then review every detail, including personal views of the foreign executive (assessed level of trust, integrity, etc.).

Once again different cultural approaches results in misunderstandings and ill feelings. Frustrated Americans spend considerable amounts of time trying to figure out who in the Chinese delegation will ultimately make the business decision. Meanwhile, Chinese delegations are often not only confused when they meet with only one individual from the American team, but the Chinese group spends a considerable amount of time trying to figure out who this person is, where they rank in the company, what kind of moral character they have, and most importantly, whether this individual should be trusted.

Often, the different cultural approach is evident within university group settings. It would not be unusual for an American team member to take charge of the group, express their opinion and quickly declare their strategy to be the way the group should proceed. Chinese students, unfamiliar with this approach, are often frustrated and not sure how to deal with this strong personality or express their opposition to the plan. An array of strategies for Chinese students will be discussed in following chapters.

Chinese Indirect Communication Style *as compared to* American Direct Communication Style

As a rule, Americans and Chinese are on the opposite ends of the cultural communication spectrum. (We will explore communication styles in great detail in the following chapters.)

However, now is a good time to introduce a new trend. In the past, Chinese exposure to Western business was very limited. So, if a deal was to be struck, it was typically the American executive who had to adjust their behavior. Recently, Chinese interactions have become more assertive and forthright for two main reasons. One, more Chinese companies are entering the global marketplace and executives have gained more knowledge and experience with different cultures. Two, there are more *hai gui* educated executives, who have experience interacting with a number of different cultures, and they are often selected to meet and negotiate with international customers.

Chinese Start with Introductions *as compared to* Americans Who Start with Proposals

Chinese want to hear about a business partner's motives, gain an understanding of a professional's business history and generalities about why a business relationship is beneficial for both parties. Proposals and details follow later – much later. In general, Americans love to talk and Asians, when in a cross-cultural social situation, love to listen. At the beginning of building a cross-cultural relationship, interactions and communication can be one sided between the two cultures.

Americans, valuing productivity, often jump right into business discussions. Of course, many Chinese consider this rushing the process and are unimpressed by this behavior. It is a very common American mistake. The Chinese want to make sure they are building a relationship with the right business partner versus rushing into a deal and discovering it is a mistake. Americans are focused on making the deal. As a result, Chinese often see Americans as aggressive, impatient and disrespectful while Americans see Chinese as slow moving and unfocused.

Chinese Question *as compared to* Americans who want to Progress

Chinese leaders typically ask a series of short questions in an attempt to better understand the

American representatives and evaluate their motives. Americans want to negotiate a deal as quickly as possible—and then move on to the next deal. Americans value productivity and like to keep the negotiation process moving. They often become frustrated by, what they feel is, the Chinese concern with their character instead of focusing on the business deal. As a result, many Americans become impatient with a series of questions. For Americans, these questions seem irrelevant to the business process. For Chinese delegations, the American tendency to reveal and disclose offers valuable insight into the American's character.

Chinese are Enduring *as compared to* Americans who are Impatient

As the relationship develops, many Americans become impatient. After a several months of meetings, Americans often wonder if the investment of time and energy will pay off. (In typical American style of thinking, they wonder if there is an ROI.) The Chinese, on the other hand, are often content going slowly and carefully.

Chinese do not want to enter a relationship they may later regret. Before moving towards an agreement, the Chinese must fully understand all the team members and feel comfortable with the interactions.

The process experiences a series of problems based on cultural misunderstanding. For example, some American negotiators have been known to offer ultimatums after a certain amount of time. For example, "we either have a contract by tomorrow or we will look for another distributor." The Chinese do not respond well to threats and this kind of action will result in silence and often end negotiations. Although the Chinese team will do everything they can to avoid confrontation, the Americans, in this case, will have to look for another Chinese partner.

This case illustrates one of the drawbacks to the American way of doing business. A hastily made decision (typical for fast-moving Americans), such as issuing an ultimatum to a Chinese negotiating team, may have several ramifications Americans may not anticipate. In addition to possibly sabotaging a business relationship, the American group may be sabotaging their reputation within an entire industry.

Chinese want to establish a "Long-Term Relationship" *as compared to* Americans who want to forge a "Good Deal"

Americans tend to focus on the present. Strike the deal and move on to the next one. However, Chinese are focused on an ongoing long-term relationship. Chinese invest the time and energy at the beginning of a relationship to identify and find the best long-term partners. Although Americans see the value of long-term business relationships and hope a business opportunity evolves into an ongoing relationship, they are also content if the deal is a one-time-only, profitable arrangement.

No chapter on understanding Americans would be complete without reflection on the differing perceptions between East and West in the business world. Below are some good examples that shed light on what we experience from our cultural perspectives.

Discussion of East-West Perceptions in the Business World

Tim Sullivan is a cross-cultural expert who primarily facilitates communication between Asian and American clients. Many of his observations and experiences are relevant to Chinese and American cultures. Mr. Sullivan's observations are listed below and my comments follow in paragraph form.

In business interactions, according to Sullivan, Chinese executives find the following American characteristics most attractive:

1. Outgoing, cheerful and creative

2. Sense of humor

3. Speak their minds

4. Good at speeches/making presentations

5. Take care of their families

Americans, especially those in a sales position, are typically outgoing, charismatic and unfiltered in their thoughts. Some Chinese find this behavior refreshing and entertaining (typically, *hai gui* or younger Chinese), others find this type of American behavior to be undignified and aggressive (typically traditional Chinese). In addition, Americans have been taught to be creative and will often look for quick, innovative ways to make a deal work. Some Chinese like this approach; others are suspicious and consider the move risky and not well researched.

Additionally, according to Sullivan, Chinese executives find the following American characteristics least attractive:

1. Take risks lightly and make strategic decisions without fully understanding the situation

2. Overly aggressive, impatient and bossy

3. Repeat the same mistakes

4. Don't consider alternative viewpoints

5. Don't keep leaders informed

Many American business people make their Chinese associates uncomfortable because they want to move quickly. By moving quickly, Chinese see Americans as not having a complete understanding of a project. In addition, as a result of moving too quickly and jumping from project to project, Americans are seen as taking little to no time to reflect on a project and gather information (Asking: what worked, what didn't work, what can we do better next time?). As a result, Americans are seen as making the same mistakes over and over again. Chinese want to know what they can learn from the experience.

In addition, American managers typically don't have as much contact with a project as Chinese managers once a project is underway. American leaders trust those managing the project and only get involved with the project when there is a problem. Chinese see the American approach as poor follow up and irresponsible. Chinese leaders prefer to have a project update daily.

As mentioned earlier, some younger and Western educated Chinese see the American willingness to take risks as an opportunity to be innovative; however, many Chinese are uncomfortable with risk and do everything they can to avoid it. Chinese do not typically make decisions on their own and tend to work closely with their bosses and leaders. As a result, they see

American business people, who often make decisions without consulting others in their organization, as having too much autonomy.

American executives find the following Chinese characteristics most attractive, according to Sullivan:

1. Hard workers

2. Detail oriented (also listed in the "challenges" as "too detail oriented")

3. Thorough data collection

4. Strong sense of responsibility (inside and outside one's department)

5. Willingness to help

Americans see Chinese as hard working, diligent, responsible and intelligent. In addition, unlike many other cultures in a multicultural team setting, the Chinese are typically willing to jump in and do what needs to be done in order to get the job done. In particular, Chinese are perceived as particularly savvy with numbers and very sharp in the financial and accounting areas. Americans feel they can count on Chinese to do their job perfectly.

American executives find the following Chinese characteristics least attractive, according to Sullivan:

1. Don't easily trust and take significantly longer than Americans to make a decision

2. Contracts and/or intellectual property are not seen or treated with respect for the American copyright mindset or legal system

3. Unclear communication, vision not easily identified by Americans

4. Don't share information with Americans, hold Chinese-only meetings

5. Don't take adequate time to study the language and culture before visiting

Chinese are micro focused, detail oriented and believe in perfection. Americans are macro focused, believe leaders visualize the big picture and workers iron out the details. Lawyers in America are big business. Almost all work agreements require a contract and American companies often sue each other. Americans are linear thinkers—they want clear and easy-to-follow communication. Chinese are circular in thought and the format for Chinese-led presentations are often seen by Americans as illogical and difficult to follow.

The process of understanding Americans clearly involves a close look at perceptions. As we have seen in this chapter, there are a series of culturally ingrained roadblocks for both cultures. The great news for Chinese and Americans alike is that the work of recognizing these roadblocks ahead of time can open doors otherwise left locked before now. The opportunity to recognize and work with differing approaches is critical for bridging the East-West communication gaps. The following chapter explores more deeply the differing communication styles and how to best transition into a new environment.

Chapter 3

Cross-Cultural Communication Styles

There are two types of communicators: *Direct* and *Indirect* communicators. Direct communicators (Americans) are verbal, transparent, assertive, linear in thought, move quickly and as one would assume, are very direct in the communication approach. Indirect communicators (Chinese) rely heavily on body language to communicate, talk less/listen more, avoid confrontation, wait for an interaction to unfold, want to understand the players in the group before building a relationship, and look at a challenge from a number of angles before moving forward with a solution. It's important to note that communication styles can adjust, depending on the setting, to reflect a specific culture's style when interacting with others outside the original culture. As you know, Chinese can be very direct communicators when interacting with other Chinese.

In general:

Direct communicators tend to be verbal, transparent, forthright and assertive (American, Canadian, German, and Australian)

and

Indirect communicators tend to be non-verbal, passive and contemplative (Chinese, Japanese, Taiwanese and Korean).

Other examples of *Direct Communicating Cultures* include Scandinavian, Israeli, British and Russian.

Other examples of *Indirect Communicating Cultures* include Indian, Middle Eastern, Central/South American and North/Central African.

If we lined up all the cultures in the world, the cultures listed above would occupy the extreme positions on the cultural spectrum. Although the rest of the world's cultures would be between them, they tend to fall on one side or the other in the spectrum.

Understanding communication styles is vital to working with individuals who have a different background from your own. The following

American-Turkish example from my own experience outlines the dynamics between direct and indirect communicating cultures. Turks, like Chinese, are part of the indirect communicating group.

I recall being in a mid-sized American city and enjoying breakfast in the hotel's restaurant. Adjacent to me were two gentlemen, wearing suits. One was American and the other (I could tell by his accent) was Turkish. The American was assertive, forthright and his voice carried throughout the restaurant. He was bent forward in an aggressive position as he delivered his sales pitch. He talked very quickly as sweat broke out on his brow and he hardly took a breath. Meanwhile, the Turkish executive sat back in his chair and listened with little reaction. On occasion, he sipped his coffee, but said not a word. Based on the conversation, this was clearly a business deal the American wanted to quickly solidify. As the American stood, he said, "I have laid out the plan, let's go back up to the suite and sign the paperwork." The Turkish man remained seated and silently sipped on his orange juice. After about a minute, the American awkwardly sat back down and began to babble even faster and louder — once again reiterating his pitch. The reality — the American executive was derailed and he began to panic as evidenced by his heightened hand motions and booming voice. Unlike many indirect communicating cultures, Americans are typically not comfortable with silence. However, the Turkish

*gentleman, in his non-verbal and non-confrontational
style, indicated he was not willing to be forced into
making a deal. In typical indirect communicating style,
the Turkish executive wanted to digest the material and
sat silently as he pondered. As the American escalated,
the Turkish gentleman crossed his arms and shrunk back
in his chair, his body language and facial expression
indicating his displeasure.*

What many Americans don't realize is that
many indirect communicators, especially those
who come from Asia, are suspicious of fast-paced
individualistic Americans who are known for being
self-serving. And what many Chinese don't realize
is that many direct communicating culture
members from countries like the US and UK find
the Chinese process of building a business
relationship far too slow and filled with frustrating
starts and stops.

Cultures are considered to be either direct or
indirect because of generalizations based on
cultural norms and values. Because Americans and
Chinese occupy both extremes on the cultural
communication spectrum, there are fewer
exceptions to the rule.

There are a few cultures that can be both
indirect and direct communicators, depending on
the situation. India represents one of those cultures.
Although Indians are typically indirect

communicators, the culture is not on the far end of the spectrum and Indians can quickly shift roles (as a product of a caste-oriented society). For example, Indians can suddenly become very direct, verbal and confrontational if they feel they are addressing someone, regardless of culture, whom they perceive is from an inferior social class.

Another example may be those who are from indirect communicating cultures, but have been educated in the US, Canada, Australia or England (and there are many Asians, Arabs, etc. who have been educated abroad) who have become more direct and Western in their communications as a result of their environments and experiences.

Many Western nations are a product of immigration, so those studying in the US will meet many people who have a mixed background. Although Americans may have a last name that indicates they are from an indirect communicating culture i.e. Singh (India), Chang (China), or Yamaguchi (Japan), many are actually a product of a blended family—one parent is from a direct communicating culture and the other from an indirect communicating culture.

And finally, sometimes someone is not like others in their culture. I was facilitating an MBA orientation and met a Chinese student who was very outspoken and the major participant in classroom exercises. He later told me that although he is Chinese, he always felt his behavior was different than his peers and he became even more Western in his interaction style after being a tour guide for foreigners during the Olympics in Beijing.

Additionally, other factors may be generational. For example, an American student who is first generation Chinese may communicate indirectly while a fourth generation American, whose family immigrated from China many years ago, may possess a very direct and typically American style.

My priority is to, first and foremost, familiarize Asian readers with Western business culture. However, my secondary goal is to have readers better understand the world's cultures. In future academic and work environments, readers will be interacting with a number of people from various parts of the world. The path to understanding is to better relate to other cultures' challenges. The more familiar readers become with communication styles and, in particular, communication styles different from their own, the more their level of *cultural empathy* will increase.

Cultural empathy refers to understanding and relating to the challenges of cultures different from your own.

The following is an example of cultural empathy at work:

If a Chinese participant is working with a multicultural group in the classroom or the boardroom, he or she may feel disrespected by the process and be confused and frustrated by the actions of other group members. Although Chinese participants are very present—constantly assessing group dynamics and body language—initially Chinese are more comfortable being silent and allowing others to lead. However, often, Chinese participants will be overrun by an American "take charge and organize the group" action. This approach will feel aggressive and dominating. There may be a period of feeling uncomfortable as the project moves along very quickly and even a sense of feeling left out of the process. In a Western environment, all participants are expected to simply speak up and participate. If Chinese participants decide to remain silent, other group members may assume the Chinese member is not contributing and team decisions will be made without their input. If an American team member, realizing the Chinese team member comes from a culture not familiar with a fast moving team process, stopped the decision-making process, smiled and softly said to the Chinese member, "I know this process is new for you, what do you think is the best way for us to proceed?"-- this would be a culturally empathetic gesture.

Direct communicators in the group may seem aggressive to Chinese participants, but direct communicators feel they are assertive and simply expressing their opinion. And how do these direct communicating Americans, Brits and Germans perceive cautious, slower-paced Chinese, Taiwanese, and Japanese behavior in a group setting? Americans often perceive Asian silence in groups as passive-aggressive or even hostile behavior. Most Americans will initially wonder why Asians are not participating, but will then focus on the project, assume the indirect communicators are not engaged, make decisions for the group on their own and ignore the non-participants.

Let's look at the dynamics. Americans, as citizens raised in a society where "All men are created equal." often feel comfortable expressing their opinion. In addition, Americans often equate strong leadership style with high productivity. However, the Chinese see quality leadership differently. From the Chinese perspective, a slow methodical process holds more importance than productivity as the main path to success. The Chinese have to establish trust and a relationship before expressing their opinion and engaging with a potential business partner. Additionally, Chinese executives feel they need to intuitively understand the members in the group. Furthermore, the Chinese culture does not have the "we are equal" approach and members who are seen as having the most experience and social status are the first individuals to start a conversation. This is because those with more experience and social status are seen as superior to those with less experience. Both cultures see their approach as better. The result: a "stand-off" and lack of group cohesion and progress.

In China, strategies on how to proceed with a challenge often take great amounts of time and a thorough examination of the repercussions of each decision. "If we choose option A, B or C, what would be the advantages and disadvantages of each decision?"

But, in American business, the priority is to keep moving ahead. Americans are often forgiving if one makes a mistake. In fact, American leaders love innovation and frequently encourage their team to take risks. "We tried that and it didn't work. Let's try another approach." is often heard in American companies. However, in China, Chinese look at every decision from all angles before moving ahead. As a result, Americans typically see Chinese business as slow to make decisions while Chinese often see Americans as a group who makes strategic decisions quickly and carelessly.

Interestingly, it is not merely a few select Asian cultures who perceive American leaders as overly hasty and quick to make decisions. Although the

US and Germany are both direct communicating cultures, many German executives consider the American decision-making style as overly focused on productivity with too little emphasis on intelligent process and quality decision making. By German standards, America's business obsession with experimentation is often considered too risky. In contrast, many American executives see the German decision-making style as too detailed, laborious and cautious.

In an American company, the executive responsible for a portion of a project is expected to know his or her segment of the project inside and out—but anything outside of their department is typically not considered his or her concern. In America, parts of a project outside one's department are left to executives in the other departments. However, in a German company, every senior executive expects to be briefed and is expected to be knowledgeable about every aspect of the project—not just what is transpiring within their own area. In addition, when leaders convene, it would not be surprising for each executive to question and directly ask other executives detailed questions about their segment of the operation. In other words, each German executive often takes on the role of a project leader for the entire endeavor.

Yet, generally speaking, in the US, if an executive were to question another executive (of similar rank, from another department) in detail about their segment of the project, it would be perceived as hostile, aggressive and inappropriate behavior. In the US, executives tend to be territorial in regard to their departments and take on a "mind your own business" reaction or "you take care of your department, I'll take care of mine" attitude if, and/or when a peer questions them.

I have included this example because it's important to understand that although cultures may have the same direct or indirect communication style, each culture often has different ways of operating. As this example illustrates, although Germans and Americans are both direct communicators, they have business styles that are unique to their cultures.

In addition, although China and Japan are both Asian cultures and have similar indirect communicating styles, each country has elements that are both similar and unique when it comes to business interactions. For example, although both Chinese and Japanese typically do exhaustive research on potential individuals and corporate business partners (especially from other cultures), the Japanese tend to rely more heavily on business processes such as root-cause analysis when formulating a strategy.

Now that a foundational awareness of the cultural background and a working knowledge of direct versus indirect communication styles is laid out here, what is needful in order to succeed in a Western academic and/or work environment?

Here are five tips to make the transition into the new environment:

1. **Commit to a Western learning format.**

   There is a good chance participants will be working in groups and with other students from all over the world. Everyone will have to make adjustments in order to work with those who come from cultures different than their own. Think about cultural empathy and try to understand the challenges others are facing and how to build bridges of understanding within a multicultural setting.

2. **Become more vocal.**

   In a Western academic and work setting, participants are expected to participate. Participation grades are common practice. It will be crucial to speak up and say what is on your mind. Make statements that are to the point, clear, logical and concise.

3. **Adopt a new mindset.**

   Assertive = Respectful. It's a difficult transition for many Asian participants. Regardless of gender, ethnicity, age or experience, everyone has an equal voice in the group and is expected to politely provide their opinion. Here are some suggested ways to enter a group conversation: Say "I have something I would like to add" or "I think we should consider this," then clearly and directly verbalize your opinion in a couple of sentences.

4. **Challenge others.**

   You can challenge others if you disagree with their opinion and say it directly but politely. Statements like, "I think there may be another way to approach this" or "I think your idea may work, but I wonder if another approach may work better" are helpful ways to express different opinions. Follow up this statement with a clear and short two or three sentence overview of your idea. Get together and practice with others until you become comfortable in your new role.

5. **Avoid "birds of a feather."**

   In the US, there is a saying, "Birds of a feather flock together." In other words, people from the same background tend to interact with others of the same background. It's a natural phenomenon and many Chinese students in the US interact primarily with other Chinese students. Chinese students can maximize their international experience by interacting with people from other cultures. Choosing to take advantage of this opportunity provides the chance to build meaningful global relationships. This book provides the skill set to better understand people from other parts of the world. Interacting with other cultures in and outside of the classroom may be a bit uncomfortable at first, but it will be a tremendous learning opportunity to evolve into a sophisticated "citizen of the world."

It's clear how different communication styles can affect cross-cultural communication. In the next chapter we will explore how different cultural approaches to decision making can also be an obstacle to communication.

Chapter 4

Conflicting Norms for Decision Making

Between East and West, there are major differences in the decision-making process. Most American members of a group, regardless of social status, gender, race, etc., typically feel they have the right to participate. In the US, one of the main parts of the country's laws is referred to as "freedom of speech." As a result, you will often find Americans voicing their opinions and challenging others. However, that is not the case in many other cultures, including China.

Although the following example is a case study of an American company operating in Korea, the same scenario could have happened if the Korean company in Seoul was actually a Chinese company in Beijing.

An American multicultural company had a supply chain issue at their main manufacturing plant. The company plant, just outside of Seoul, was way below output goals and the company's vice-president in the US, after a number of conference calls, was not able to get to solve the problem. The Korean team had been vague in their description of the problem and the vice-president decided to send one of his most capable staff members, an operations specialist, to take care of the problem. The woman he decided to send to Seoul was a tall, overweight redhead with over thirty years of domestic US experience in supply chain operations. Upon her arrival in Seoul, she immediately called a meeting and conveyed her agenda—as she would have done in the US. She ran the meeting as she would have done in the US. Without introducing herself, she demanded a full report from each of the local executives that afternoon. None of the executives showed up for the afternoon meeting. When the US executive went from office to office looking for the executives, they could not be found. In addition, none of the emails she sent to the Korean team were acknowledged. As her frustration level escalated, she pounded her fist on desks and loudly demanded secretaries tell her where she could find the team. All of the secretaries avoided the American executive and many acted as if they could not speak English or understand her. After a ten day stay and no progress, she returned home. A week after her departure, the supply chain glitch was solved by the Korean team and business resumed as normal.

As you can see, there were several mistakes made in this scenario. The female executive approached the situation with little cultural sensitivity. If she had known about and been able to respect cultural differences, she would have taken two days just to establish a relationship and create a foundation for communication. The American approach of identifying the problem and instructing a team to quickly fix the issue simply doesn't work in many parts of Asia. In addition, sending a tall, large, loud, strong-featured woman with a red bouffant is not in sync with the Asian business gender, appearance, and attire norm. It sabotaged any sense of familiarity and created a wall of distrust. And finally, in typical non-confrontational Korean style, the Korean team simply avoided and shut out the foreign participant until she finally left in frustration. However, in due time, and on their own timetable and their own way of operating within a group, the Korean team solved the problem.

The truth is there are a number of cultural ways to approach challenges and accomplish goals. It is important to start thinking like a global leader. How would you handle a similar situation? For example, what kind of individual or team would you send to the US if leading a Chinese company experiencing problems at a US manufacturing plant? Use cross-cultural knowledge to select recruiting or international teams with precision. Pick the most culturally savvy players to not only represent you and your company, but the appropriate cultural fit for each situation.

The Chameleon Factor

The key to building bridges in new environments is through cross-cultural awareness, understanding the audience, knowing how you are perceived, and then adapting your behavior accordingly — much like a *chameleon* which changes colors in order to survive. Anyone can build rapports and levels of trust by adjusting actions, dress, body language and voice tone to put others at ease. Now I am not at all suggesting anyone shed his or her identity. I am simply suggesting Asians (and any other culture adapting to a new locale) will build stronger personal and professional relationships by adopting a chameleon mindset.

A friend from college is a perfect example of how a cultural chameleon can thrive in the business world. He had carved out a middle-class existence as a real estate agent in Long Island. In 2007, when the real estate bubble exploded, he quickly became desperate. His business had fallen apart—he had no listings or buyers. Since his income is completely commission-based and the real estate market showed no signs of recovery, he called me in a panic. I encouraged him to reframe his efforts and take advantage of the current real estate situation.

Knowing a weak domestic real estate market and weak dollar translated into amazing real estate bargains for international investors, I helped him recreate and position himself in order to appeal to the international market. He obtained a Manhattan office and address by finding a small office space, which he shared with other small business owners. He then proposed possible sales opportunities to potential American sellers by assuring them he could get top dollar for their properties from foreign investors. They had nothing to lose in a stagnant domestic market and got on board. He then took out a series of calculated ads in foreign newspapers and presented himself as the contact person and real estate authority for their US investment. He also researched the opportunities and challenges of foreign investment in the US, how investors could minimize legal and governmental hassles and made transactions easy for buyers. Those buyers then told their friends and soon he was getting more opportunities than he had expected.

He then went into what I call *cultural chameleon mode*. He learned a number of greetings and key phrases in a variety of target market languages (He already spoke German.). The result: interested clients felt at ease when they spoke with him. He practiced each phrase repeatedly until he spoke like a native with the proper inflection and accent. He researched each culture before clients arrived in New York City and knew appropriate gifts to offer (if any at all), cultural superstitions (colors, numbers) and details right down to what kind of car he would rent to show them properties (his Swedish clients were delighted he "owned" an upscale Volvo). In addition, he familiarized himself with each cultural food item and ordered for the group when attending ethnic restaurants.

Essentially, he did everything he could to make his clients feel like they were being pampered by and interacting with "one of their own." The real estate bust was the best thing that ever happened to him. His business became, and still is today, an overwhelming success. And he is the first one to tell you it is because of his ability to adapt his personality to suit the sales situation and, in essence, be a cultural chameleon.

In addition to understanding conflicting norms for decision making, Chinese students should become familiar with Western ethics and expectations - covered in the upcoming chapter.

Chapter 5

Ethics & Expectations

The academic environment in the West is more easily understood once students learn about US ethics and expectations. The following sections focus on how to avoid ethical dilemmas, such as plagiarism, and how to adapt to Western academic expectations.

Ethical Dilemma

In terms of misrepresenting qualifications or abilities, US educational leaders are very strict. This is important to know. If any student attending a Western institution is caught breaching Western integrity standards (such as cheating, lying, falsifying documents or plagiarism), they can expect to be punished and even dismissed from the program.

Plagiarism

In China, to copy someone else's words is often considered a compliment to the author. Recreating someone else's work occurs often and is not perceived as unethical or improper. This is in direct contrast to the US. Plagiarism, or copying someone else's work and presenting the work as your own, in a US academic environment is not tolerated. It is thought of as being much like, if not exactly the same as, theft. Unlike China, in American society, submitting someone else's work as your own is often dealt with severely.

During my work at a US university, I heard about a Chinese student who was caught in what Americans consider an unethical situation. He downloaded and copied an entire paper from the Internet and submitted the work as his own. Because the paper was so well written and the professor knew the student's English was not as fluent as was presented in his paper, the professor did his own research on the Internet and discovered the same paper the student submitted — word for word. Once the professor reported the incident, school leaders called in the student and confronted him. The student refused to admit he didn't write the paper. School authorities showed him the overwhelming evidence on the Internet and yet, the student still refused to admit he copied the paper. Even after he was released from the program and returned to China, he claimed he was wronged and a victim of a set up.

Being familiar with Chinese culture, the student's action of copying the paper and his denial reaction when caught are not surprising to you. Many Chinese students who venture abroad feel tremendous pressure to succeed. The temptation to submit a perfectly written paper is often difficult to avoid. It is a very risky decision and often ends very badly with students being sent home. Regarding his insistent denial, to admit he cheated and then, as a result, was excused from the program was a profound disgrace for both him and his family—so he had to stand by his story.

In this case, many American administrators and students could not understand why the student reacted the way he did and would not admit he had copied the paper. Many Americans are not familiar with "losing face" and the shame that goes along with it. Beyond basic honor and pride, maintaining "face" avoids disgrace for the individual and their family, which is paramount in Chinese culture. Most American students would admit, when faced with the evidence, that they copied the paper and ask for leniency when caught in this situation. They would then have a chance of staying in the academic program at the university.

For Chinese students, the discussion surrounding ethics is often confusing. On the one hand you cannot copy another's work, but on the other hand you can take credit for a group's work if you are in the group. For example, students typically work in group settings and the group decides how to approach a challenge. Some groups break the challenge into different parts and each group member is responsible for a part of the project. Then all the parts of the project are put together by the group leader and submitted — with all of the group members' names. For one Chinese student, this caused great concern. Since he only wrote one part of the five-part project, he did not want to be accused of unethical behavior. He went to the professor and the professor assured him the group's approach was not a problem.

Plagiarism occurs only when an individual puts their name on someone else's work. Submitting a paper or project, in which a part of the submission is someone else's work, is permitted as long as the other person is given credit. In this group project example, all members' names were on the project. Additionally, the work was completed by the five group members so there was no ethical violation or problem as seen from an American perspective.

Here is another example. As part of my business, I coach student applicants and help them navigate the US application process. One of the goals in the process is to put together a well-written and compelling essay. Parents (especially parents of international applicants who are unaware of US ethics standards) often ask me to write their children's university application essay. Given the culture I live in and the resulting values I follow, it would be unethical, unprofessional and not something I would ever consider. So, I explain what I can do to support and assist their child and operate in the ethical realm. I either meet face-to-face or Skype with the student applicant. I ask a series of questions. Together, we outline and list a series of accomplishments, experiences and pivotal moments to include in the essay. Then the student writes the essay on his or her own. I then edit the essay and make suggestions. The result—a solid application essay, but most importantly, we do not violate ethical guidelines. The essay was written and submitted by the student.

China is known in the international arena for viewing intellectual property as public property or as having no distinct ownership by any one person or entity. In China, books and music are often recreated with no acknowledgement or compensation for those who wrote, sang or produced the material. Americans generally find this behavior and action unacceptable. For Chinese students, the Western focus on ethics is a whole new environment. Therefore, this section on plagiarism is vital and critically important for Chinese to understand. Take the time to read and reread it again and again. Students are not expected to perform perfectly, but are expected to always follow Western ethical guidelines. Chinese students, who are concerned about a paper or project and wonder if they have crossed the unethical line, should consult their professor for clarification before submitting their work as a final product.

Academic Interactions and Expectation

Chinese students often feel pressure to be the best. The Chinese culture is detail oriented and as a result, students are hesitant to submit a paper or project that they feel is not perfect. While there are exceptions, American professors are not as concerned with perfection and are quite forgiving. In addition, they know English is not the native language for many students. This doesn't mean Chinese students should not pay attention to spelling, grammar and context. American academics are more interested in leadership potential and thought processes—the ability for students to think with an innovative perspective and solve problems intelligently and strategically.

Many Chinese students are accustomed to school officials and professors looking out for them and individually helping them each step of the way. This does not happen in a US academic environment. There is no such support. Although professors typically have office hours (a schedule when they are in their office and available for students) a few hours during the week, these meetings are called "drop-in" sessions. Drop-in sessions are designed to be very short—not more than a few minutes long—and an opportunity for a student to ask one or maybe two questions.

Typically, American curriculum moves quickly and students are warned not to fall behind. In fact, many classes have work that is expected to be completed prior to classes even beginning. Professors may cover several chapters of material per week and often give unannounced quizzes during the semester. In China, some students receive special attention because of their family name or social status. Chinese students should not expect that in the US. Professors are concerned with how students perform not their family name or social status. In general, American professors treat students equally.

Another potential area of adjustment for Chinese students is formality. China is typically a formal society whereas America is informal. In China, students typically address professionals by their title: "Doctor," "Professor" or "Mr./Mrs." Many Americans prefer to be called by their first names. Chinese students may be shocked to hear a professor or administrator introduce him or herself by their first name. The best way to navigate this challenge in America is to be formal. This way one will be sure not to insult or offend anyone. However, if someone prefers to be called by his or her first name, then do so. And if someone is interacting in a casual style and it is uncertain how to address him or her, it is perfectly acceptable to ask: "Would you prefer I call you Professor Smith or John?"

Protocol

When venturing to a part of the world one has never been to before, it's important to become familiar with another country's traditions, customs, rules and expectations.

As an American, accepting an invitation to visit a university or place of business in China presents numerous opportunities for considerable success or embarrassment. The difference between those two extremes—success or embarrassment—is defined by the level of investment made beforehand in understanding cultural expectations. For example, several years ago, I accepted an invitation to present at a university in Shanghai. During my two-day visit, I counted over 30 social mistakes I could have easily made as a Westerner—from how to present my business card to gift selection/presentation to how to toast at a banquet.

In general, the protocol requirements for professional and respectful interactions were many.

Chinese students in a Western country and/or on a Western campus may find themselves making adjustments in order to succeed and avoid embarrassment. There is typically tremendous support available. American academic administrators and staff members are often very helpful in assisting international students make a smooth transition to a new environment. The best way for Chinese students to easily transition to a Western environment is to recognize and respect America's academic expectations and ethical standards.

Chapter 6
Levels of Fluency

Most people know fluency to be how well they can speak a language. Unfortunately, some people confuse fluency with intelligence. This often happens in the West. American, British and Australian students are at a distinct advantage in the global arena because many meetings are conducted in English and many Western students do not have the experience of being surrounded by a language different from their own. Chinese students often feel hesitant to speak English because of their fluency level. In addition, some Western students may confuse a Chinese student's lack of fluency with being unintelligent. In facilitating a number of cross-cultural focus groups, I have had the frustration of witnessing brilliant participants suffer the embarrassment of being ignored because of an inability to verbalize input clearly in English.

When speaking to native English speakers about fluency, I always include the following points. For one, I remind native English speakers to put their "cultural empathy hat" on in a multicultural, yet Western-focused environment and speak slowly (without coming across in a patronizing manner), ask open-ended questions, and avoid overly technical words. Also, it is beneficial for participants in a multicultural group to ask questions to clarify: "Ling, when you said _____, what did you mean?"

In addition, non-native English speaking students will be better served to "feel the fear and do it anyway." This is a common adage in the US. Certainly many non-native English speakers are hesitant to directly speak to native English speakers and some are absolutely petrified to speak in front of a large group. It's natural and understandable to be afraid. Nobody likes to make mistakes and invite embarrassment. This can be particularly true for Chinese students who often set very high standards for themselves and never want to "lose face" or feel disrespected by others. However, when it comes to another language, practice makes perfect.

Here are some tips to become fluent in English.

1. **Download a translation application on your smart phone.** As a backup, carry a dictionary and notepad with you. When you hear an English word you do not know, either look it up or write it down (so you can look it up that evening). Although initially you will be looking up or writing down words constantly, you will find yourself understanding more and writing less as time goes on.

2. **Avoid "birds of a feather"** and regularly interact with other native English-speaking students. Ask native English speakers to join you for lunch or meet for coffee. You will find Westerners to be very friendly. Don't be afraid to ask questions (For example: "Excuse me for interrupting you, but you said the word _____ - what does that mean?").

3. **Immerse yourself in your new culture**. Fluency doesn't come about just from speaking, but also by listening. The more you put yourself in English-speaking venues such as restaurants, malls, stores, sports events, etc., the faster you will become knowledgeable of not only proper English, but of often-used slang.

4. **Ask for input**. When interacting with native English speakers, ask them for help. For example, in Western graduate schools, students often work in teams. You can say to your team, "I am working on perfecting my English and would appreciate your help. If you hear me say a word incorrectly or make a grammatical error or use a word in the improper context, please let me know so I can learn. I will not be offended and will welcome your help. Thank you." If you open the communication door with this statement, you will find your team to be supportive and helpful.

5. **Embrace media.** Watch television and go to the cinema. The more you hear and see Westerners in action, you will become more familiar not only with language, but with customs and traditions

6. **Find an English speaker who wants to learn Mandarin/Cantonese.** Many native English speakers, especially those visionaries who recognize the emerging importance of China's role in the global economy, are anxious to learn your language. Teaching your language to native English speakers will enhance your English fluency level.

7. **Live with Americans**. Moving to another country can be a scary and intimidating experience. Having a Chinese roommate may bring you comfort since you share the same customs and traditions. However, realistically, you will learn English much faster if you are surrounded by the English language at home as well as in school. Consider your academic experience an adventure and seek American roommates.

How Do We Define Fluency?

In general, the idea of fluency is not easily measured. Are any of us ever really fluent in a second language? Learning another language is an ongoing process for everyone. It's sometimes impossible to determine a point at which we can say our vocabulary has evolved enough to be able to claim fluency. Those whose language of origin is English discover new words in English on a regular basis, yet they consider themselves fluent.

In spite of years of experience and practice with more than one language, I can personally relate to having the fluency rug pulled out from underneath me. A few years ago I was contracted to do some short-term consulting work with a French company. During the interview, which was conducted in English by a non-French speaking interviewer, I confirmed my knowledge of French.

However, I could not follow the conversation during meetings and had to eventually excuse myself from the project. My knowledge of French is purely conversational and when it came to French business words (like "leverage" and "strategy" or business terms like "data sets," "marketing profiles" and "business plans"), I found myself only understanding bits and pieces of the conversation. It was at that point that I wondered — how do we define fluency?

My personal opinion about fluency and how to define the term is best summed up in this way: We are fluent in a language when we can think in that language. Up until that point of transition within our brain, we tend to think about a phrase or word in our native language and then we translate it. As we become more fluent, the translation time decreases. Then there is that magic moment when we can think and speak in that language. It is that moment that defines fluency.

When facilitating orientations for US graduate schools, I often find Chinese students saying over and over again, "I am so sorry for my English." My response, which typically makes people smile, is: "Your English is so much better than my Mandarin. I am delighted you are here and you are an important addition to the team." It's not something I say to be polite. It's true.

Chinese students are typically intelligent, disciplined, eager to please, friendly, respectful and work well with others. China is positioned to become the leading economic superpower in the world. Many business leaders predict Mandarin will eventually be the dominant language in many global corporations. Meanwhile, Chinese students should not let their current lack of English proficiency hold them back—attending university in the West will provide the opportunity to quickly become fluent.

In addition to understanding how language fluency impacts intercultural relationships, students can benefit from understanding how social strata and hierarchy affects relationships within and between cultures.

Chapter 7

Perceptions of Hierarchy

"Perceptions of hierarchy" refers to how a culture sees or experiences hierarchy. "Hierarchy" refers to how a culture ranks members of their own society according to a number of factors, including status (gender, education level, age, and family background). Many Americans don't recognize how social strata and gender often affect intercultural dynamics. For example, the Indian culture is very caste sensitive; but many other indirect communicating cultures, including Chinese, are also affected by hierarchical perceptions.

As mentioned previously, one of America's values, "all men are created equal," creates an environment where Americans feel comfortable voicing their opinion. Certainly there are some times when this is not the case. For example,

Americans may be aware of their status in a company such that a manager may be hesitant to publicly disagree with a vice-president's decision. However, Americans generally do feel comfortable expressing their opinion. In fact, many American middle managers feel compelled to speak out when in the midst of senior executives. The mid-level executives view the opportunity as a chance to impress the senior executives. This behavior is also seen in academic environments. American students tend to be outspoken and want to impress their professor. In fact, many professors provide a portion of a student's grade based on class participation levels. However, in China, executives and students alike tend to take a more passive position, assess the players and selectively participate. In general, Americans encourage and expect everyone, regardless of age, gender, social strata or experience, to participate.

Another example regarding different perceptions of hierarchy in China: The oldest and most experienced member of a team will typically be the first to voice his opinion and set the tone. The reason for this is simple—as far as the Chinese culture is concerned: It would be considered disrespectful for a more junior person to disagree with an experienced, senior member. And that attitude and sense of respecting elders and their experience in the field extends beyond China and throughout most of Asia. In the US, it would not be unusual for every student or executive to take on a leadership role at some point during the semester or employment tenure.

Hierarchy affects many industries within each culture. Although the following illustrative example is Korean, the same scenario could have just as easily occurred on a Chinese or Japanese aircraft. Several years ago a Korean airliner, preparing to land, was far short of the runway. In addition, even though the first officer knew they were on a path to disaster, he was reluctant to express his opinion and question the older and more experienced captain's lead. A questioning subordinate would be considered disrespectful and would cause the captain to "lose face." The first officer remained silent as the plane crashed into the English countryside, several miles short of the runway. In the US, when faced with the same situation, there is a good chance the less senior pilot would have warned the senior pilot and taken action to avoid the disaster.

Gender also plays a dominant role in cultural communication. In traditional Chinese work environments, women, typically, are not permitted to play a leadership role. Men often dominate upper management and women often carry out the instructions. I have seen this time and time again in Asia. Women—typically only one, maybe two at the most—sit in silence in a group meeting. The men discuss strategy and when a decision has been reached, one of the men turns to the sole female member and assigns her to carry out the task.

There are several indications that this trend may be changing. One is a huge increase in female university enrollments. Many believe a new generation of ambitious Chinese women is emerging.

But the change isn't just amongst Chinese women. It appears Chinese men are more tolerant of female leadership. Many younger Chinese men are more open to working alongside females than their parents' generation. Although playing a secondary role is the current cultural business norm for many women in Asia, it appears women's roles and status are evolving and from all indications, evolving quickly. Many international business leaders predict Chinese women will soon be a major force in the business arena.

So how do Asian women adjust to an equality-minded American environment? A friend of mine is a very accomplished Japanese woman who lives in the US. She has been in New York for over thirty years and has built a solid and profitable cosmetics company. When we interact, she is very American in her behavior—assertive, outspoken and demanding. However, I had the opportunity to see her in action while interacting with Japanese executives and her attitude was completely different. She was proper, elegant and soft spoken. She used her charm and language abilities to build trust and negotiate with Japanese associates. Of course she had a distinct advantage with her Japanese clients because of her appearance and language abilities. Nonetheless, she uses her *cultural chameleon* skill set and adapts her personality to accomplish her business goals.

When interacting on the global stage, it's important to be aware of certain political situations and world history. These dynamics can also play a role in hierarchical perception. Several years ago, I was facilitating a seminar for Asian executives. The title of the seminar was "Understanding American Business," and naturally included a section on differing communication styles. Within the group, there were two large sets of Chinese and Taiwanese executives. I made the mistake of presenting both cultures in the same sentence—"Chinese and Taiwanese cultures have the same indirect communication style." I immediately sensed the entire group stiffen and disengage. Members of the group had misunderstood my example and thought I was suggesting the Chinese and Taiwanese were the same people. I quickly called a break and although I was aware of the political tensions between China and Taiwan, I didn't realize putting both cultures in the same communication style category would cause such a problem.

The most important part to remember in this chapter is this: in an American academic or work environment, you are on even ground with others. You have no advantage or disadvantage when compared to others in your group. Gender, background, social position, age, which part of China you come from, work experience or any other defining factor that may or may not make you feel special or not special are not something to rely on for an advantage. You have to prove yourself and make your mark based on your merit and performance.

Of course you are a talented and intelligent academic who wants to be prepared for your new environment. There is a strong chance you will be in classes and working on projects with students from all parts of the world. In your new academic environment, everyone will be considered equal and the following exercise will help you start thinking this way.

The question to dwell on for this exercise is "How open-minded am I?" This question is by no means a criticism or judgment. I find it interesting how Americans automatically react when discussing prejudice. The immediate and politically correct response is: "I'm not prejudiced." But it's just not true. All of us are prejudiced and there is no shame in harboring prejudices. All of us learned various thoughts and attitudes about other groups as we matured. But we can become more aware by acknowledging our prejudices, identifying where they came from and then make a conscious effort to see how our prejudices might be limiting personal growth. To that end, I've devised a three-step process. The following exercise is a worthy investment of your energy and will quickly move you down the "Citizen of the World" experience curve and firmly entrench both feet on the ground as a centered, self-aware global leader.

Open the door to greater awareness with the following three-step process:

1. **Acknowledge:** The first step is quite easy. You just have to acknowledge you are human and that, as an inevitable fact of being human, you harbor prejudice but are willing to embark on a journey to rid yourself of restricting thoughts about other groups of people.

2. **Trace:** The second step is to trace what you think about other groups and identify what your conscious or subconscious may feel about groups or individuals who may have different backgrounds from you. For the purposes of this book, circle the globe and

think about ethnicities different from your own. Start with China's neighbors in Asia (Japan, Korea, Philippines, Singapore, etc.) and expand from there. Then start generating a list of countries from all continents you may have some knowledge or thoughts about (ex: Americans, Canadians, Swedes, Thais, Nigerians, Mexicans, Australians) and write down the first reaction that enters your mind when you think of these groups. Be honest with your responses. You are the only one who will see your answers.

3. **Explore and Challenge:** The third step dives even more thoroughly into your self-analysis. Ask and answer two critical sets of questions as shown below in order to explore and challenge prejudice:

> ➢ Where did my thoughts about other cultures originate? Did my beliefs about other cultures come from my parents or grandparents? Community? Teachers? Religion/Philosophy? Media? Did I get my impression of a certain group of people from an article I read in a newspaper or an international movie or television show? Is my impression of a group of people from my own personal

interaction? Did it enter into my thinking via another source?

➢ How can I take myself to a different level and become more open to people from other cultures? How can I identify and appreciate the best others have to offer? Even if other groups behave differently than I do, am I willing to be open to the idea that another cultural approach or thought process might work better?

Although this is a short chapter and exercise, it is critical. Take the time and sit with your thoughts. You will get out of it what you put into it, and much more. Keep in mind that as the author of this book I encourage all students, regardless of their background, to undertake this very same exercise. We can work together to respect, appreciate and understand our differences.

Chapter 8

Going West

American Culture

It's important to note that America, like China, is a large country with a number of regions. Each region has its own demographic makeup and personality. Just as living in Shanghai would differ from living in Xian, living in San Francisco is different from living in Dallas. Depending on where you go to school, you may find differences in speech, slang, body language and appearance. In addition, certain parts of the country tend to be more conservative or liberal. Some universities are in large cities—others are in small college towns. In addition to selecting your school based on ranking and reputation, you may want to consider location and quality of life factors in the decision-making process.

At this point you are:

a) Preparing to graduate from high school and attend an American university <u>or</u>

b) Preparing to graduate from a Chinese university and attend an American graduate school program.

Remember Jiang—the depressed and lonely Chinese student I described in the introduction of this book? In addition to looking at grades and test scores, recruiters are looking for students who will fit in socially. Some schools require interviews as part of the application process. Interviews are being designed to identify and eliminate students who are not willing to adapt to a Western environment and admit students who are a good social fit for the school (especially for students who are applying to programs that require interaction, like an MBA or HR program). Certainly you know what to expect when it comes to questions about your academics – those questions will be direct and clear. But you may not know what to expect when recruiters are trying to evaluate your personality type.

Campus "Culture Fit"

The next section includes the type of questions more and more American recruiters will be asking. These types of questions are designed to probe your ability to think critically, understand your emotions and know yourself. These types of questions are difficult to prepare for or memorize because there is no right or wrong answer. It's about you as an individual—your personality and how you see your life experiences. Understanding what you feel, how you feel and why you feel a certain way is a cultural priority in the US. Unlike your possible approach to other interview questions, you should not try to memorize an answer—recruiters will see right through your strategy. Your level of sincerity and self-awareness will be evident if you take the time to think about who you are, what makes you unique and why you like your personality **before the interview**.

American recruiters believe applicants who are self-aware and willing to explore outside their comfort zone are the best candidates. Recruiters are looking for future global leaders who want to learn, grow and explore. Besides considering smart and well-educated candidates, recruiters want to admit students who are able to relate to and interact with people from all backgrounds.

Sample "Culture Fit" Questions:

> ➢ What is one of your favorite books or movies? Which character did you identify with and why? Which part of the book or movie made you angry or sad? What

experiences in your own life reminded you of those same feelings?

➢ What is your favorite memory and tell me all about it. How did you feel during the experience? Why do you think this was such a special time? Do you know of anyone else who had a similar experience? Do you think they felt the same way about it? If not, how do you think they felt?

➢ Who is your favorite relative or friend? What is it about this person that makes them special to you? If they could use three words to describe you, what three words do you think they would choose? If I asked them to name one part of your personality you should change, what would they say?

School Selection

The following sections cover various factors and opportunities Chinese students can consider for their best chances of success.

Out of the colleges or universities that have accepted them, Chinese students typically attend the ones that are rated the highest. Most look at the school's ranking whereas factors like location, campus life, student diversity, climate or access to Chinese restaurants, churches and clubs are not as important.

Another major factor in college selection: Many Chinese students will attend a school where they already have friends in attendance. It's called the "multiplier effect." As more Chinese students attend US universities, their friends and classmates often apply to the same school they attend. Some US universities have found themselves receiving hundreds of applications from Chinese students who all live in the same location. Since this will create a Chinese community, there is more of a likelihood that Chinese students will only socialize with Chinese friends. As a result, they will miss out on a multicultural experience.

It's really about finding a balance between cultures. Although I hope you take advantage of the experience and immerse yourself in the Western cultural experience, my wish is for you to also maintain contact with other elements of China and Chinese culture. It will keep you from getting homesick—especially during the first few months of your transition. There will be times when it is nice to touch base with the familiar, like a Chinese meal you cook with friends or lunch in a restaurant or on campus with Chinese friends.

Here is my suggestion—keep an open mind and think about not only which school is the best for you academically, but which school will be a good fit for you socially, a place where you can stay linked with your heritage but also explore and grow as an individual. This may or may not be a school with a large number of other Chinese or international students, but may be accessible to at least some element of a Chinese community.

So what is life in the US like and how can you select the right school and part of the country for you? It's a difficult decision—especially since you may not be able to visit the campus prior to enrolling. As you know, campus visits are expensive (airfare, lodging, food) and not necessarily in the budget for many students.

US Culture

It's difficult to describe a diverse country like the United States—there are many regions and each has a different personality. However, the following information may help you narrow down your search.

Regardless of where you go to school, there will be many local holidays along with summer, fall and spring breaks during your stay. During the breaks in which you don't return home to visit family and friends, take advantage of the opportunity and visit different parts of America. This type of interaction is an education in itself and will broaden your ability to understand another culture by socializing with a cross-section of Americans. In order to familiarize you with different parts of the United States, review the following information regarding different regions.

Let's start with America's largest city, New York City. Many Americans think of New Yorkers as loud, competitive and argumentative. But many others have found New Yorkers to be compassionate and make special efforts to help others. There is one thing most can agree upon when describing New York City: the city is busy. New York City is the throbbing heartbeat of American business—from Wall Street to Broadway and Madison Avenues. If you like a fast pace and being in a high energy city, you should research schools like Columbia and NYU.

California is a huge state with different personalities and reputations. Southern Californians (Los Angeles and San Diego) are seen as fitness oriented and drawn to a more leisurely lifestyle. If this type of atmosphere is appealing to you, research The University of Southern California (USC), Pepperdine University or the University of California at Los Angeles (UCLA). Northern California is the home to ultra-liberal and sophisticated San Francisco and preppie Palo Alto/San Jose. For the former, research the University of California at Berkeley and for the latter, look at Stanford University.

Texans are often seen as eager to impress and very proud of their Texan heritage. In fact, Texas once had an ad campaign that said, "Everything is bigger and better in Texas." Like California's major cities, Texas has many different personalities. Houston has an established oil industry and a number of diverse communities. Dallas is more conservative than Houston and home to banks and insurance companies. And then there's liberal Austin, which is known for its technological industries. Houston is the home to Rice University; Dallas features Southern Methodist University and Austin, University of Texas.

Southerners are known for being hospitable. Personal relationships are valued and strangers are noticeably polite to each other in stores or passing on the street. The south is known for a slower pace, but as in all the regions, there are many exceptions. For example, sophisticated and progressive southern cities like Atlanta are fast paced and savvy. If the south appeals to you, research Duke University or Tulane University. If a more urban atmosphere in the south is appealing, consider Emory University in Atlanta.

Washington DC is certainly one of America's most diverse cities with a number of cultural centers and a large international diplomatic community. If a sophisticated locale appeals to you, consider George Washington University, Georgetown University or Johns Hopkins University (in close-by Baltimore).

Charming, yet cold, Boston has more colleges per capita than any other American city. A number of top schools are in the Boston area, including Harvard and MIT.

Many consider those who live in the Midwest as the most mainstream Americans. The central part of the nation is typically flat, farm country (most notable exception is Chicago—a major financial and cultural center) and people in this region are generally friendly, reliable and honest. If elegant, yet chilly Chicago is appealing to you, research highly touted University of Chicago and Northwestern University.

There are many types of campuses—from urban to college towns. If you feel you would fit in best with a highly intellectual crowd and have outstanding credentials, you may want to focus on the Ivy League schools in New England such as Dartmouth or Yale or University of Pennsylvania in Philadelphia. If you feel you may be more comfortable in a university dominated "college town" atmosphere, research universities with large international student populations like Purdue University in West Lafayette, Ohio State in Columbus or University of Michigan in Ann Arbor.

When selecting your school, of course your first criteria should be academic. However, I suggest looking at the complete school profile. There are many factors to consider and you may be accepted to schools with similar academic reputations. In that case, perhaps the other criteria may help you make your decision. In addition to a school's academic reputation, you want to look ahead towards graduation and how well prepared the school is to assist you in your career (placement rates and the quality of the career services department).

Choosing a school is a big move. You are about to make a commitment for several years and you want to be happy and comfortable. There are hundreds of great schools in the US to choose from—you can find one that meets your needs. It's important to keep in mind that for all the generalizations about each region of the US, there are exceptions even from one city to the next. Most importantly, regardless of which school you select, know your experience will also be what you make it. Go into this next life chapter with a positive attitude and meet as many other students as possible.

Language

In America, there are lots of accents and dialects. People from NY speak fast. People from the South speak slowly and say "y'all," "sir" and "ma'am." People in New England are often quieter and speak little. Young people from casual southern

California often call each other "dude" and say "you guys" when addressing a group. Midwesterners also do not have as much of an accent as Americans in other parts of the country and as a result, many national telemarketers have set up offices in the Midwest.

Immigrants

America is a land of immigrants and many have built communities. There are heavily Hispanic cities like San Antonio and El Paso in Texas; almost half of Caribbean immigrants live in the Northeast—around Boston and New York City. Asians have flocked to San Francisco, Los Angeles and Seattle.

Additionally, some cultures tend to be visible in certain industries. For example, in New York and Los Angeles, Koreans are often greengrocers, owning small fresh fruit and vegetable stores. In the Silicon Valley (Northern California), many Indians work in the software development industry while many Russians drive taxis in New York City.

Looking Down the Road

For now, Chinese students have several career options upon graduating from an American university and more options will become available as the Chinese economy grows internationally.

Upon graduation from a Western university, Chinese students can work for a Chinese company in China (or for a Chinese company abroad — as more Chinese companies expand internationally, this will become a more common option). Or perhaps Chinese graduates will secure a position with a Western or multinational corporation abroad (with a company willing to sponsor them). Some students may obtain employment with a multinational company's Chinese division. Some may decide to become entrepreneurs and build their company and life in China or abroad in the US, UK, Canada, Australia or another country. In short, a Western education creates opportunities with a number of appealing options.

Graduation from either undergraduate or graduate school is on the horizon and you want to interview for an exciting new position as a global leader in a Chinese or multinational corporation. How can you prepare for interviews? The following is a basic outline of interview protocol.

Basic Interview Protocol:

Prior to Interview

1. Research the company.
2. Identify proper formal business attire.
3. Make sure your phone is off.

During Interview

4. Shake hands with a firm, confident handshake.
5. Maintain eye contact with one or both interviewers (if two interviewers, try to engage each of them equally).
6. Take a moment to think before you answer.
7. Ask one, maximum two appropriate questions (see Question section below)

After Interview

8. Present and ask for a business card
9. Send a personable, hand written thank you note to the interviewers

After Interview Questions – Appropriate and Inappropriate

Appropriate:

- Question how the company/interviewer distinguishes a great employee from a good employee.

- Question what else, in addition to what is listed in the job description, the interviewer can tell you concerning the job (Include something you have learned about the company from online research when formulating your question. It will show you have a great interest in the company.).

Western Culture

Inappropriate:

- Questions about the interviewer's background

- Questions asking information you can find online

- Questions about pay, benefits and/or time off

- Questions such as: "How quickly can I be promoted?" or "How quickly can I start applying for internal positions?" or "How long before I can transfer to a Chinese branch?

Career Opportunities for Asian Students

US employer surveys reveal most recent graduates (students, including domestic and international students) are equipped with the workplace competencies they need. However, recruiters report many graduating students are not able to articulate and demonstrate their abilities in job interviews. For non-native English speakers, this challenge is even more difficult—especially for those who have not made the effort to interact. However, many non-native, English-speaking graduates receive multiple job offers with multinational corporations. The key to their success: most of these successful students (like Wei) strategically immersed themselves in Western culture and their studies. After one year, they were fluent in English, able to present their thoughts and experiences (in English and Mandarin) and confident in their abilities. However, for some students (like Jiang), US companies report the potential for cultural misunderstandings and additional training costs are too high to hire these types of Asian graduates.

Here is some feedback from corporate recruiters. Their input is for all students preparing to enter the workforce, not just international or Chinese graduates. An August 2013 study conducted by Northeastern University revealed students with a global perspective and those who had studied, traveled or worked abroad are more successful employees. College recruiters seem to agree. When asked about the skills they are looking for during the hiring process, 83% of corporate recruiters report a desire to identify and hire professionals who are culturally competent and prepared for a globally interactive work environment. However, when business leaders were asked to rate the quality of overall US graduates, two-thirds of executives believe college graduates are not prepared for the global economy.

These trends create an opportunity for international students. In particular, Chinese students studying in the West have cultural knowledge and experience in at least two key global parts of the world — China and America.

These experiences and, in particular, the ability to manage multicultural teams is what international students need to relay and capitalize on in an interview situation. It is a sure way to impress recruiters. Although Chinese students may feel other native English-speaking applicants have a fluency advantage, Chinese students have a highly valued skill in their multicultural business perspective and multilingual ability. Chinese students should not undervalue their Chinese background. China has incredible potential with many opportunities. If I, along with many other visionaries am correct, China is poised to be the dominant economic superpower.

Interviewing

Interviewing can be a stressful process. However, interviews can be even more difficult when English is not your first language. The key is preparation. As mentioned earlier, your career services department will guide you—but here is some additional information.

Career Services

Career services is a vital part of university programs and can help you find your dream job. Many schools are seeking out companies who want to hire and sponsor international graduates, while others are growing their international network in an effort to increase international hiring opportunities. Some schools have even developed career services divisions dedicated to international students. In addition, many business schools have included a career management class in the curriculum which requires students to attend lectures by leaders working in their field of expertise i.e. marketing, finance, accounting etc. These lectures often include a number of suggestions for international students and, in particular, how to get a job with their company.

When selecting a school, look closely at the school's career services division and ask the following questions: Does the university have a separate and dedicated staff to support for foreign student job seekers? Do the schools schedule "how I did it" presentations by successful international students who secured jobs in the US, China or another country? Do they organize job hunt trips to China (in order to meet with prospective multinational and Chinese employers)? Does the school offer webinars to address cultural gaps and identify companies that are more open to sponsorship?

The following question may be the most important one: **How innovative is the career services division?** For example, one university with a large business school links students with short-term consulting jobs that allow them to stay and work in the US while they look for a full time position. This valuable experience, particularly popular in the private equity and banking industry (working on analytic and financial projects), allows students to continue their job search.

Many career services divisions in the US (and UK) ask students to make a decision prior to graduation so they can make out a plan for the student. The students are asked to select one of three paths: seek a job/sponsorship in the US; seek a job with a multinational corporation in China; seek a job with a Chinese company in China.

Entry Level Positions/Sample Interview Questions:

Most of the interview questions will be about your academic knowledge and abilities. Although you or your peers will probably have comparable levels of knowledge in your field, you can make an impression on recruiters by employing PAR/Q, shown below. This is where you need to be a *cultural chameleon* and very Western in your communication. Recruiters want direct answers that are logical, clear and concise.

P—Identify and recap the **Problem**

A—The **Action** you took to rectify the situation

R—Outline the **Results** of your action

Q—Quantify your response, if possible, by providing data in your answer to prove your point.

You will have to create your own responses based on your experiences and what you think. The following are just samples to consider:

Tell me about a specific situation in which you encountered a work related problem and how you overcame the obstacle?

Last year I interned at _____ company. Sales unexpectedly dropped 25% in Japan. After analysis, the team I was a part of determined that consumers reacted negatively to the product's ad campaign. The ad that was in place was an American ad with a poor Japanese translation. After replacing the ad with a Japanese production, sales exceeded expectations. In fact, the new ad resulted in a 40% increase in revenue.

In addition to these types of questions, there may also be a section of the interview designed to gain an understanding of who you are as a person, your interpersonal skill set and your ability to be respectful, yet direct and assertive.

Describe to me a specific situation where you had a conflict with a colleague and how you dealt with it?

On a project, I was partnered with a student who ignored me and dismissed my input. I arranged a meeting with him to discuss my concerns. During this discussion, I told him I felt ignored and asked him if there was a particular reason for overlooking my input and told him that I wanted to participate. He denied there was a problem, but from that point forward, we were able to build a strong working relationship.

Non-Specific, Open-Ended Questions/Sample Responses

Many interviewers use an "open-ended" question format (questions that are not simply answered by a yes/no response) to see where you, as the interviewee, take and direct the conversation. This is an ideal opportunity to introduce your cross-cultural skill set and knowledge. The key is to relay to the interviewer that you are prepared for the global marketplace by highlighting your talents— you are multilingual, assertive, clear, have a multicultural knowledge base and want to bring global best practices to your new employer.

Examples follow.

1. **What is the most important thing you learned during your time at _____ university?**

Attending _____ university has been a life

changing and broadening experience. In addition to being academically prepared, I now have a greater understanding of Americans and how they conduct business. I immersed myself in the American culture and have a solid understanding of American norms and values. In addition, my language skills have improved tremendously, and I feel comfortable conversing in English.

2. What did you learn from your internship at _____ company?

In addition to gaining valuable practical experience in _____, I learned a lot about myself by working with a variety of peers from different cultures. Additionally, I had the opportunity to manage multicultural teams. As a result, I gained valuable experience effectively communicating and leading key players who come from other cultures. I now feel confident and comfortable working in both Western and Eastern work settings and can be a bridge of communication between cultures.

3. Why do you want to work for our company?

I see your company not only as an industry leader, but also as a multinational company that is positioned well for growth. I am confident of my ability to interact with peers around the world and will thrive in your company culture. I feel I could be an asset to your organization as you expand within China.

4. What would you say is your biggest accomplishment in your career/life? Why?

I see my biggest accomplishment as my willingness to expand my perspective and become a global citizen. I am confident in my ability to overcome culturally-based communication obstacles. As a result, I am a solid team player, considered a strong leader and know how to effectively interact within both Western and Eastern cultures.

5. How would you describe your personality?

I would characterize myself as open minded, competent and flexible. I work well both individually and in a group setting. In particular, I enjoy working with a diverse group of peers and am a team player who is known to build camaraderie and unify teams. Culturally, I am a chameleon. I feel very comfortable interacting in the US because I have lived here and in my home country of China because I grew up there.

6. How would you describe your interaction style in groups?

I thoroughly enjoy group projects and, in particular, I thrive in multicultural group settings. I welcome all members within a diverse group and believe in achieving global best practices. During my time at _____ company, I had the opportunity to participate in a number of cross-cultural projects. I bring the best of both Eastern and Western business practices to the group setting. I believe, as Westerners do, in being productive and innovative and as Easterners do, in being thorough and detail oriented.

Keep in mind that you should not memorize the sample interview responses and use them as your own. These are just examples so you can get an idea of what you might want to say. You will need to create your responses based on your experience. The key is to be honest. It will not serve you well to say you managed teams you did not manage or participated in cross-cultural projects that did not happen. As much as you feel any alterations of actual history might help you convince a recruiter that you are a good fit for the company, it's important to protect your credibility. A recruiter will do a thorough background check on you. If they find what you told them not to be true, you will no longer be considered for the job.

Chinese Students: How to Get a GREAT Job

Depending on the university you attend, there will be varying levels of interview preparation provided by the career placement team. Universities are very aware of academic rankings — all of which include a series of job placement-related components. As a result, many universities are putting a great deal of effort into insuring you are ready to effectively interview and receive job offers that pay well.

However, much of that information is designed for the graduating class as a whole and is not culturally specific. The following are some tips, observations, ideas and experiences you, as an Asian student, can benefit from:

1. Be honest.

Recruiters are typically savvy and intuitive. In addition, they know some students will say what they think the recruiter wants to hear instead of voicing how they really feel.

Here is a classic example: I heard a story about an on-campus recruiter who interviewed a Chinese applicant from a top MBA program. She asked him questions to get a sense of his learning capabilities. He responded that he liked to read and had read lots of books. She asked him what kinds of books he had read. With a broad smile, he told her he had read business books his professor had recommended. She asked him the name of the title or the author. He said he couldn't remember. She then asked him about the insights from the book. The student then became nervous and told the recruiter he hadn't yet read the books because he was so focused on his coursework. The interview quickly ended and the student was not hired. Once the student demonstrated a lack of integrity, he lost his opportunity.

2. Write and practice your elevator pitch.

An elevator pitch is a short sales pitch (called an elevator pitch because it should be short enough to say on a short elevator ride from one floor of a building to the next floor) that provides a potential stranger with information about you. You would use your elevator pitch at events like career fairs when you might only have a minute to impress a recruiter. The information you reveal should be concise, informative and interesting. In addition, it should include some tidbit of information that will help you stand out from other applicants. Elevator pitches are typically no more than five sentences. Think it through and memorize it. Every word is important.

3. Research how to prepare an accurate and impressive resume.

Professional resumes always begin with an executive summary. Recruiters review thousands of resumes—this is your chance to stand out. Grab the recruiter's attention by writing a dynamic executive summary that reveals your best attributes and accomplishments. Just make sure you are accurate and don't add events or attributes that don't belong in your summary. This way you avoid awkward or embarrassing situations. The executive summary will give the recruiter the incentive to continue reviewing your resume. Unfortunately, far too many students do not include this important piece of the resume. You don't get a second chance at a first impression — put together a solid and concise executive summary before laying out your resume.

4. Network, network, network!

In addition to LinkedIn (mandatory), join other job-related social media sites.

5. Utilize campus career centers.

Campus career centers are free and typically have a number of resources. Some would argue they are not really free since you paid for these services with your tuition. So since you indirectly paid for the service — use it! Make friends with the career placement staff. It can help you immensely!

6. Practice interviewing.

Ask others for honest and constructive feedback. Constantly assess and revise your interview strategy

7. Put a short list together.

Create a list of the companies you want to work for, then research each one and the jobs they have available. Let the company know you want to work for them and why they are at the top of the list. When preparing for the interview, strategically list specific examples that not only demonstrate your skills and abilities, but prove you are a good fit for the job. Let the recruiter know you are passionate and excited about working for the company.

8. Contact key individuals at companies where you want to work.

Prepare a well-written email and direct it personally to the leader within the appropriate department of the company. Most leaders, especially Westerners, are impressed with individuals who are assertive and take the lead. Let them know who you are (your executive summary), and why you want to work for their organization. Then ask their opinion (leaders love this!) about how to make working for their company a reality. Conclude by thanking them and asking if they have a few minutes to speak on the phone or meet you for coffee.

9. Talk with your favorite professor to get leads.

10. Show passion and personality.

If you are interviewing with an American firm, focus on being upbeat, conversational and assertive.

11. Make your responses insightful and powerful.

Practice your elevator pitch; think about what you want to project, what will make you stand out and how to deliver that message with short, clear and well thought out responses.

12. Be able to present your credentials verbally.

Basically, know how to relay your executive summary in just a few sentences. The select few sentences should relay your career goals concisely and clearly

13. Smile and maintain good eye contact.

Common Interview Mistakes:

- Lack of passion: Avoid a lack of passion by having, understanding and conveying the motivation or reasons you want the position.

- Not fully prepared for the interview: Avoid lack of preparation by researching the company thoroughly.

- Not sharing specific examples to prove behaviors: Avoid lack of proof by having real examples of accomplishments. Prepare for interviews by listing accomplishments and specific moments or interactions that created an opportunity for learning and growth.

Executive MBA/ Senior Level Executives/ Sample Questions

Executive search firms seeking enthusiastic and visionary senior leaders often have an entirely different interview style and approach. You can anticipate these kinds of questions if you are at least a director in a company and graduating from an Executive MBA or MBA program. The assumption is made that applicants on this level have the skill set, so questions are designed to identify leadership abilities. Questions are a bit more abstract and may include the types of questions shown in the following sections. Also, I include questions that are on the fringe or which might seem extreme in order to give you an idea of how far out of the norm these questions may be. Recruiters know those who have worked in the business world are experienced interviewers and may ask some of the following types of questions in an effort to solicit honest and spontaneous responses. In addition, I have supplied some sample responses.

Example questions and responses follow:

1. **If today were the last day of your life, what would you do?**

After ensuring everything was in place for my work successor, I would spend the day with my family.

2. What are you most interested in and speak most enthusiastically about?

Excellence and supporting my team in our pursuit to be the best.

3. What do you want others to remember you for?

My ability to lead in an honorable and ethical manner.

4. What do you enjoy most about leading people?

Helping them realize their potential.

5. What do you enjoy most about sales?

Helping bring people together with the things that will make their life better.

This chapter provides plenty of thought-provoking material and exercises to help Chinese students prepare for the global marketplace. Building a solid professional network, discussed in the following pages, is another key element to success.

Chapter 9
Network Building

The Chinese and American approaches to finding a job, increasing business or making new contacts are completely different. In the US, one does not rely solely on intermediaries to network. Rather, Americans build a network and constantly connect with new individuals (through interactions, conferences, telephone and via internet) in an effort to increase their scope and network of connections. Although some people still collect and catalog business cards, most professionals now use social media to build their network. The most trusted, respected and utilized social media outlet for business professionals is LinkedIn.

Do you remember the "Return on Investment" in the first chapter of this book? One of the points outlined by Chinese employers is *haigui*'s lack of local Chinese connections or "*guan xi*." LinkedIn can help you overcome this obstacle and build your network not just in the West, but also in China. More and more Chinese are embracing LinkedIn—not only those who study and/or work in the US, but those who study and work in China. I strongly urge you to create a LinkedIn profile if you do not already have one. This chapter will show you how to create and/or perfect your LinkedIn presence.

LinkedIn is a massive gathering space for business professionals. It is especially popular in the US but growing exponentially worldwide. The site has 259 million members in over 200 countries. LinkedIn offers professionals a chance to hone and increase contacts—all for free. You also have the ability to limit your connections to others in a particular field, so you can focus on those individuals who can best help you professionally.

The key to success with LinkedIn is to keep your profile current and to stay connected. Ignoring connection requests or connecting with the wrong people can make the site and your efforts pointless. Many professional fall short and don't maximize LinkedIn's benefits by staying current. You can be the exception.

LinkedIn Basics:

➢ You have the opportunity to create a compelling text and narrative of your life and work. In essence, the LinkedIn profile is the current generation's resume. Once you sign up for LinkedIn, you will be guided through the process of creating your profile. Write an extensive profile that speaks of your strengths, skills and experience. You may also add multimedia, such as slide presentations and links to examples of your work.

➢ Use the headline space (right under your name) to create a compelling statement about yourself. Instead of "Graduate Student," be creative. "Bi-Lingual Marketing Professional with over 3 years experience Managing Multicultural Teams" will generate more views.

➢ Look up high visibility profiles of individuals with backgrounds similar to you. What keywords did they use to generate traffic to their profile? Consider using any of the same keywords that apply to your own experience. (This is not unethical. Keywords are not individual intellectual property and are used commonly depending on how they are relevant to the individual. No one owns the rights to a keyword and they are available for anyone to use.)

➢ Add a professional photo. Data shows adding a photo to your profile will increase (by 11 times!) the chances that recruiters will click on your profile. Another tip: if you list more than one professional position, you will increase your visibility search by 12 times.

➢ LinkedIn will automatically let all your contacts know every time you change your profile. Your colleagues will receive an update when you change jobs or add additional experiences. Even if you only change the title of your existing job, your network will receive an update via computer.

➢ Place your cursor over your picture in the upper right. Click "Review," next to "Privacy and Settings." On the "Profile" tab, you can turn off "Activity Broadcasts" (notifications to your network every time your profile changes) or decide who in your network can see them if you decide to leave them on. This is the same spot where you can select filters: you may choose to let others know if you have viewed their profile (or remain anonymous), how much of your profile strangers can see and even send automatic updates to your Twitter account (along with other features).

➢ If you are looking for a specific job, here is a tip to catch the interest of recruiters. In addition to keeping your profile up to date, add new accomplishments and suggested news articles in the "Share an Update" field at the top of your home page.

➢ You should only link with people you know. However, on occasion, you may receive an invitation from a stranger. How should you handle that situation? I suggest you reach out to that person and schedule a phone or Skype call. During the communication, see if there is not only a reason to create a professional relationship, but make sure both of you share the same business perspective.

➢ Join interest groups. You'll find them by searching for names and key words in the search bar at the top of the screen. Once you join a group, you can offer advice, share contacts/news articles and express your opinion. When you comment in groups, you will build a reputation and your name recognition will spread. Here is a tip when you begin your job search: join discussion groups that focus on companies at which you might like to work. If a job opens up, you will then be able to connect with company executives you have become familiar with during conversations within the group.

➤ You will also notice another LinkedIn feature called Endorsements. Endorsements were designed so LinkedIn participants can endorse particular skill sets of those within their network. For example, if you think someone within your network is an excellent trainer, you would "endorse" that person by clicking "training" on their profile. However, endorsements hold little credibility with professionals and recruiters. In fact, many believe the endorsements feature will be eliminated.

I suggest you build your profile immediately and invest the time and energy required to insure you are professionally profiled on the LinkedIn global stage. Building your network and staying in touch with contacts is key to success in the global business arena. However, building a quality network is of no use unless you leverage your connections.

Asking your professional connections to help you network or connect you with decision makers is often uncomfortable, but particularly uncomfortable for Chinese. For many Chinese, asking others for help contributes to "losing face."

But in the US, contacting your connections and asking them to help you is quite common.

This is how it works. People reach out to their connections via email and say something like:

Hi John,

This is just a quick note to touch base with you. All is well here and I hope this message finds you and your family (if you know and have met his family members, include their names here) healthy and happy.

Additionally, I want you to know I am looking for a job in (Marketing, HR, Finance, etc.—put as much detail in here as possible, for example, "a job in International Finance with a Fortune 500 company") and would appreciate your support. My resume is attached— (include a quick recap, "I have solid work experience with _____ company, am tri-lingual and getting my MBA from _____ university). If you could link me with any of your connections who may be looking for someone with my background, I would certainly appreciate it.

As always, hope to see you soon and sending my best.

Sincerely,

There is no reason to be embarrassed or uncomfortable. You are not asking for a job, you are asking for the opportunity to secure a job. The rest of the process, such as interviews and then doing a great job if you receive an offer, is up to you.

Chapter 10
Where Do We Go From Here?

Now is the ideal time to not only recap some of the highlights of this book, but also to ask you to consider if and when Chinese, American or other cultural approaches might be best suited to a particular situation or challenge. This line of thinking or discussion may not be comfortable for you, but these kinds of conversations and discussions are common in a Western academic environment. Western universities are designed to create critical thinking and capable leaders who can direct people, solve problems and be innovative when seeking solutions. Besides, isn't true global leadership what you want to strive towards? True global leaders have an expansive way of thinking and embrace global best practices.

The following points from earlier chapters will give you some cultural perspectives to think about and discuss with your peers.

Cultural Consideration 1

"In fact, American leaders love innovation and often encourage their team to take risks. 'We tried that and it didn't work. Let's try another approach.' is often heard in American companies. However, in China, Chinese look at every decision from all angles before moving ahead."

Both cultures' approaches have their merit. In what situation is one culture's approach better than another? What would be the result if American business adopted a slower, more analytical Chinese pace? Might the new approach save time, money and aggravation in the long run? What are the benefits and flaws of researching repercussions of decisions from each and every angle before implementation?

On the flip side, how could a more American business approach benefit China? Would Chinese productivity levels increase? Would increased tolerance for risk also increase levels of innovation?

What do you think? An American academic system teaches students that there may be no clear, correct answer. The reasoning for these types of questions is to develop your leadership ability and critical analysis skill. You, as a future global leader, are expected to justify and clearly present your strategy and vision. Ultimately, you may contribute to your company's success or failure—so it's vital for you to look at the positive and negative outcomes of each decision.

Cultural Consideration 2

"American, British and Australian students are at a distinct advantage in the global arena because many meetings are conducted in English…I have had the frustration of witnessing brilliant participants suffer the embarrassment of being ignored because of an inability to verbalize input clearly in English."

Certainly there is an advantage to being a native speaker. But how will this change as other cultures, such as China, grow in global markets? As Chinese companies expand internationally, will meetings at headquarters be conducted in Mandarin or Cantonese? Will native-speaking Mandarin and/or Cantonese leaders be receptive to input from international employees? How will language abilities be an advantage or disadvantage as Chinese companies grow and prosper? How can Chinese companies invite and value input from all employees, regardless of ethnicity or language ability? How can Chinese companies embrace international employees who may bring valuable input to the organization?

Cultural Consideration 3

"Many Chinese students are accustomed to school officials and professors looking out for them and individually helping them each step of the way. This does not happen in a US academic environment. There is no such support and it is often considered 'hand holding,' which is not part of the academic culture."

The US is an individualistic culture. China is a collective culture. What are the benefits of each academic approach? While the US encourages students to respectfully work in teams, the academic structure also teaches students to work independently and competitively. In China, professors and administrators nurture students and guide them through the learning process. Which approach do you think is best and why?

Cultural Consideration 4

"The Chinese have to establish trust and a relationship before expressing their opinion and engaging with a potential business partner. Additionally, Chinese executives feel the need to intuitively understand the players in the group."

According to many of my American colleagues, business is not to be confused with friendship and many Americans don't feel the need to evaluate a business partner's ethics or know much about their personal lives. In addition, Americans feel protected by the legal system and, in particular, the American emphasis on contracts. Striking a deal with someone of questionable integrity is not always a concern for Americans since both parties are bound by law.

However, many analysts believe ethics should be a consideration and a part of the business conversation. Regardless of contractual protection and guaranteed compensation for work, do upstanding executives really want to be affiliated with an underhanded individual or organization? What does that say to employees, suppliers and other customers about levels of integrity?

For many, the Chinese approach of doing business with only credible partners has its merit. Many Asian cultures, including China, will do exhaustive research on potential American business associates before conducting business. If Chinese executives discover an affiliation with questionable partners, they will either not do business or will at least approach with additional caution. The bottom line—many believe linking up with questionable individuals or companies may benefit business in the short run, but may cost in the long run. What do you think?

Cultural Consideration 5

"In fact, many American middle managers feel compelled to speak out when in the midst of senior executives. The mid-level executives view the opportunity as a chance to impress the senior executives. However, in China, executives and students alike tend to take a more passive position, assess the players and selectively participate."

This is an interesting observation and speaks to the American tendency to value those who are outspoken and take center stage. As mentioned earlier, the Western academic program values participation and often a portion of a student's grade is based on participation levels. However, it is important to think before you speak. All too often the outspoken individual, in an anxiety-provoked desire to make a positive impact, blurts out an inappropriate statement or comment, which, in a matter of seconds, damages their reputation.

Cultural Consideration 6

"It would be considered disrespectful for a more junior person to disagree with an experienced, senior member. And that attitude and sense of respecting elders and their experience in the field extends beyond China and throughout most of Asia."

Inviting and valuing the input of an experienced executive is often overlooked in youth-focused

American culture. An American executive, in their mid-50's, can often be considered no longer valuable. Executives in this age group, well aware they are in a vulnerable place, can become skittish and avoid the limelight. The executive's goal at that career crossroad is, all too often, to stay below the radar until retirement. Additionally, many older executives are exhausted from the corporate pace and disappointed with politics within American corporations. On the other hand, many Chinese executives in the same age range are at their best. Their wisdom is respected and they are often the spokesperson and leader of their team.

How can the Chinese prepare themselves to encourage American business leaders to learn to move towards valuing depth, experience and knowledge?

Cultural Consideration 7

"There may be a period of feeling uncomfortable as the project moves along very quickly and even a sense of feeling left out of the process. In a Western environment, all participants are expected to simply speak up and participate."

I see it time and time again. Americans often volunteer to be group leaders and Chinese participants take a secondary and passive role. How can you change the cross-cultural dynamics and become more comfortable in a leadership position?

Chinese students can politely and respectfully interact with direct communicators in their group. If a direct communicating culture member, like an American, is dominating a group, ask the American to slow down and consider the possibility that other members of the group can also offer valuable contributions. You can then encourage Americans in your group to talk less and listen more. In addition, you can teach them valuable tactics from your culture—for example, how to be more aware of body language and other non-verbal communication clues.

Each group and project is different. It's really about growing your *cultural chameleon* personality. Sometimes a take-charge approach is needed by you or another group member and sometimes you may be better served by taking a quieter support role. Trust your intuition.

Cultural Consideration 8

"She was proper, elegant and soft spoken. She used her charm and language abilities to build trust and close the deal with Japanese associates."

Many Americans reacted to the above scenario by suggesting my Japanese friend was manipulative and false when projecting her Japanese self. I disagree. She is multi-faceted and her personality is not flat. She simply put another aspect of her personality forward (in this case, her Japanese self) because her intuition told her it would be a good fit for her audience. She made a great decision. It was a brilliant, profitable and ethical move. Chinese students can also work between both worlds, East and West, and put those personalities into play when appropriate. In fact, understanding both East and West is a valuable asset. As global citizens, we can all be flexible, dynamic and intuitive in life and still operate from a place of integrity.

Cultural Consideration 9

"'Chinese and Taiwanese cultures have the same indirect communication style.' I immediately sensed the entire group stiffen and disengage. Members of the group had misunderstood my example and thought I was suggesting the Chinese and Taiwanese were the same people. I quickly called a break and although I was aware of the political tensions between China and Taiwan, I didn't realize putting both cultures in the same communication style category would cause such a problem."

This is a good lesson for all of us to note when you have potentially warring groups under the same roof. In order not to offend, be particularly cautious and choose your words carefully. In this case, it was Chinese and Taiwanese. But this lesson could be applicable for a number of groups, cultural and non-cultural alike—from Indians and Pakistanis to Christians and Muslims who may be housed in the same forum.

Analyzing Cultural Considerations

It's important to ensure this book looks thoroughly into how to help differing cultures adapt and accept a variety of perspectives.

For example:

1. What part of a hierarchical structure is valuable?

Could one argue the years of both life and professional experience are worthy of respect and more experienced opinions and contributions should be given priority and special consideration? Should groups who only have basic information regarding an organizational challenge defer to the older and seemingly wiser members of a group for a strategic response until the challenge facing the group becomes clearer? As a Chinese student, this thought is easily understood. Take it further and ask how you can explain the value of a hierarchical structure to Americans.

2. What part, if any, of America's equality-centered value is potentially narrow-minded or lacking?

Could one argue equality-mindedness, while essential to avoiding judgment and maximizing participation, does not always foster awareness of limitations? Additionally, does equal mindedness discount the wisdom and insights of others who possess more knowledge or life experience? And finally, does equality foster an environment that obstructs the motivation to cultivate skills or areas of expertise by lumping people under one label? How can you help Americans understand where their own values could obstruct progress?

3. Which parts, if any, of China's "slow methodical process" or America's "full speed ahead" form the most valuable approach and how does your opinion change, if at all, from small groups to large organizations?

These are interesting questions for you and your team to discuss and, of course, many more cross-cultural points to debate, like:

- Are we evolved to the point where we can entertain the possibility that another culture's "flaw" may be the solution to one of our cultural obstructions or setbacks?

- Would the adoption of other cultural perspectives bring a greater sense of balance and position to China and America, resulting in future success?

This conversation goes both ways. For example, would a Chinese corporation, firmly set in a formal operating mode, benefit from the looser American "go for it" approach and if so, how do you think changing the business norm and rules would be received by employees?

All of these questions are open to debate and do not have definite right or wrong answers. Although you may firmly believe one approach is best, your perspective may change as you hear others present their arguments. Additionally, your answer may change based on the situation or details of a particular scenario. For example, a number of variables, including company size, industry and target markets may affect your decision.

As you have probably surmised by now, the goal of all these final questions and the purpose of this book is to not only prepare you for a Western academic experience, but to open your minds, expand the realm of possibilities beyond Chinese and American cultural limits, and encourage you to start thinking like a global leader.

You may now be a Chinese student, but after your experience in a Western university, you will be able to think and debate like a global leader.

You can embrace the best the world has to offer, logically identify what approaches meet individual and organizational needs and then make *Global Best Practices* a reality. You are on the road to establishing a strong and respectful presence in the global marketplace by becoming culturally skilled in thought, actions, behaviors, and attitude.

Acknowledgments

To J. Ruth Kelly, my amazing manager and social media assistant, whose guidance and diligence keeps me focused, my respect.

To Kristine Putt, my talented brand consultant who creates with vision and innovation, my admiration.

To Charles Collins and Susan Manahan, two insightful editors who analyze manuscripts with incredible patience, my gratitude.

To Adina Staicov, a brilliant cross-cultural authority and resource, my appreciation.

To all of you, inherently gifted in your own unique way, my loyalty and thanks.

www.ingramcontent.com/pod-product-compliance
Lightning Source LLC
LaVergne TN
LVHW011240080426
835509LV00005B/572